Concept for EP

EPCOT Center Construction

Derek Walker
EPCOT 82

EPCOT Center Conceptual Model

EPCOT Center Construction

It is interesting to back-track a little before describing the latest Disney spectacular which is to be unveiled to the public in October this year, because what we will see then is not quite the EPCOT (Experimental Prototype Community Of Tomorrow) that we were led to anticipate in early days when Walt Disney outlined the plans for the newly acquired 27,000 acres in central Florida. At that time the plan to be developed over time offered the following components:

• A complete 'Vacationland' opening in October 1971 (which it did) encompassing theme resort hotels, Motor Inns and campsite accommodation and featuring a wide variety of land and water recreation facilities
• Within this Vacation Kingdom a family theme-park similar to Disneyland in California
• An entrance and reception complex to receive and welcome all guests
• An 'airport of the future' offering service to private and executive aircraft as well as commercial commuter service
• An Industrial Park designed to showcase American industry at work
• A transportation system carrying guests from place to place and linking the many attractions of Walt Disney World
• And finally an Experimental Prototype Community of Tomorrow (EPCOT) where Walt Disney said **'People actually live a life they can't find anywhere else in the world today. EPCOT will be a "living blueprint" of the future...a fully operating community with a population of more than 20,000. Here American free enterprise will constantly introduce, test and demonstrate new concepts and technologies years ahead of their application elsewhere.'**

That, sadly, has not happened with the EPCOT Center. American industry's enthusiasm, though prepared to underwrite many experimental and innovative techniques in communications, transportation, agriculture, energy and science, believes these innovations should be demonstrated as industrial showcases in participatory exhibiton form rather than in the Utopian setting indicated in earlier literature.

In essence, therefore, EPCOT is another gigantic themepark. It has taken two distinct and perversely contradictory themes - Future World and World Showcase - as the generator for its formidable array of attractions. The logistics of the enterprise numb the critical faculties by their extraordinary scale. Master planning of EPCOT only started in 1976, on a 550-acre site. Three thousand designers and 4,000 construction workers are involved in the venture. The 1,800 artists, designers and engineers at WED Enterprises are backed by over 1,000 consultants in the multi-faceted and often innovative design programme. The construction management is by Tishman Construction and there are nine major

contractors on site with specific responsibilities for the pavilions and a further seven on site developing utilities and energy systems. The budget of $800,000,000 more than doubles Disney Production's investment in the Florida site.

Dynamic theming is the language of Future World. Major corporations representing a variety of industries have linked their best creative thinking to the entertainment talents of the Disney organisation. The eight major presentations of Future World are:

• Spaceship Earth presented by the Bell System - a spiralling journey through the interior of an eighteen-storey geosphere. The history of communication is traced from the first cave images to computers whose electronic pathways take you to the very edge of space.

• The Universe of Energy presented by Exxon will take you through the great geological upheavals that enfolded fossil fuels deep within the earth, up to the present and on to examine the energy sources of the future. Presentation uses the most complex film system ever developed. The pre-show is projected onto 100 rotating triangular screens with periactoids.

In another theatre guests will see the largest piece of animated film ever produced on a giant screen 150 ft wide. This, together with a multitude of special effects, including Disney's latest offering, would you believe 'smell', makes Huxley's 'feelies' in Brave New World just one small step away.

The roof of the energy pavilion will have a six-acre area covered with 80,000 photo voltaic cells in 2,200 modules - the world's largest private solar installation. The system will produce 70,000 watts of DC power which will be used to drive six electric passenger vehicles, each carrying a section of the Energy Show audience; each vehicle will carry 100 passengers.

• The World of Motion presented by General Motors is three shows in one - a zany ride through the history of transportation takes guests to Centercore, a six-storey-high kaleidoscopic view of a futuristic city and to Trans-Centre, the showcasing of advanced concepts in present and future transportation systems.

• The Journey into Imagination, presented by Kodak, is the Fantasyland of Future World - a voyage through the creative process should be a riot and participation enables latter-day Leonardos to show a little temperamental excess in the electronic factory optimistically called Image Works. Naturally, after all this action, sedation is at hand in the Magic Journey Theater, which screens the largest three-dimensional motion picture ever produced.

• The EPCOT Computer Center presented by Sperry Univac showcases the systems that keep Disney World operating smoothly. It is intriguing to see at first hand the overlay of showbiz that enables this feature to be personably entertaining rather than chillingly menacing.

However, the two most intriguing areas in one's introduction to EPCOT are aspects of two pavilions, the structural language and space utilisation of the geosphere and the Merle Jensen contribution to the Land pavilion. The Land, an enormous Future World attraction, the size of Tomorrowland in the Magic Kingdom, is presented by Kraft. A major ride through the attraction, with boats carrying 2,000 guests an hour, travels through three agricultural areas - desert, aquacell, and a tropical region. In the presentation, some 150 crops that the world depends on for food will be grown side by side with superstar plants of the future and some unique new growing methods for food production systems will be shown for the first time. These leafy sentinels are part of the experiment being carried out by Merle Jensen in his environmental research laboratory at the University of Arizona. They allow crops to grow vertically rather than horizontally, to be fertilised by constant nutritional spray (like a car wash), and to be exposed to light and shade necessary for maximum growth potential. The result is often twenty times the normal crop. The stars of the show are really the systems. The technique of hydroponics is demonstrted, as is a polyculture system where aquatic animals and plants grow one above the other. Intercropping is demonstrated by growing pineapple plants next to papaya trees, with sweet potato plants interspaced. Adjoining the area Chinese cabbages grow out of styrofoam boards, but undoubtedly the two most interesting exhibits are halophyte plants that survive and even thrive in a brackish or salt-water environment (a potential solution to the world's food shortage), and the Buck Rogers exhibit where lettuces grow in a spinning aluminium drum simulating space agriculture.

Spaceship Earth provides a less exotic challenge, but as the first geodesic structure to achieve a complete sphere encompassing 2,200,000 cubic feet of space, it certainly posed intriguing structural and general arrangement problems. A 165 ft diameter geosphere poses some very interesting questions about weather-proofing, with tons of water plunging down from the globe's 'equator'. A globe-girdling gutter was developed to collect the water at midpoint and channel it through the structure and its supporting legs to underground drains. The dome is two separate spherical structures, one inside the other. The inner sphere is composed of 1,450 structural steel members arranged in typical geodesic form. The inner core also contains decking at several levels, and a spiral route for Spaceship Earth's ride system. It is covered by a waterproof membrane to protect the inner workings. The outer sphere is held 2 ft away from the inner core by aluminium hubs and contains aluminium support frames for 954 triangular aluminium panels. The upper portion of the dome's interior becomes a giant projection screen where a planetarium effect is achieved - one of the largest such show surfaces ever created.

The structure serves as housing for the ride system and each leg becomes a part of another structure housing service and show functions.

The two rear legs become a part of the Earth Station, the City 'Hall' of EPCOT Center. It houses the world's Key Information System, an electronic guest service network. The ride system track is 1,520 feet long. It accommodates 152 guest vehicles and 76 spatial effects vehicles. The cars rotate as necessary for maximum impact of show scenes.

Ascending the spiral trackway the ride vehicles, holding four passengers each, finally emerge into 'outer space', then rotate 180 degrees, descending backwards down a slanting ramp structure.

It is perhaps churlish to criticise a yet unfinished EPCOT at an architectural level, but for all its brilliant showmanship and internal excitement it shows the uneasiness in handling future technology as built form that Tomorrowland has always shown in the Magic Kingdom.

It is significant that the truncated fragments of the old world's civilisation draped loosely round yet another man-made lagoon offer the ultimate one-day trip round the World. The pity is that for many they will become a substitute for the real thing.

One gets very worried to read in current Disney literature: '**Like an impressionist painting, this photograph captures the magic quality that surrounds the World Showcase pavilions. Each country in miniature will be so authentic in detail that a tour will leave you feeling you've experienced the real thing!**' Piazza San Marco without San Marco! England knee deep in Pearly Queens! and Germany swilling in lager . . .'

Yet what can one say? EPCOT will be enormously successful, give tremendous pleasure, provide extraordinary entertainment and make serious points about the future. It will not, as many would feel, be the 'death knell' of 'imagineering' or the imagineering approach. It will perhaps quietly reinforce the view that the compactness of Disneyland and the art of the berm and landscape enclosure offer lessons to EPCOT's more grandiose approach. In essence, the character of EPCOT is more akin to a World Fair than another world, and a World Fair rarely combines innovation, cohesion and quality, even with the best architects in the world contributing.

EPCOT perhaps exaggerates this syndrome because it has been unable to remain close to the original concept. It is a demonstration rather than a realisation.

I love Disney and what he has done to stimulate the 'art' of vacation leisure, but I wish his successors could have pulled off the original concept - we could then dwell on the technological planning and social successes rather than the ephemera of brilliantly organised frou-frou that WED does by instinct.

Greenhouses

World Showcase

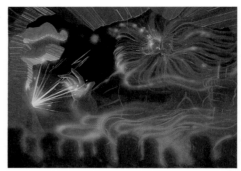

Earth Station

EPCOT Center Rendering

Construction

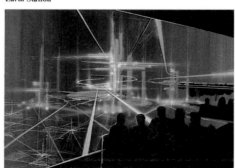

World of Motion

Spaceship Earth

United Kingdom Site

Kitchen Kabaret Show

Kitchen Kabaret Model

Audio-Animatronic da Vinci

Primeval Diorama Model

Maquette of Figment

The Living Seas

Dinosaur

Leonardo da Vinci Studio

5

The Building Process

Matterhorn Skeleton

As the EPCOT Center nears completion for its opening date in October 1982, it is interesting to document the sheer scale of building activity undertaken by the Disney Organisation in the last thirty years.

1952-55 covered the master planning and building of Disneyland in Anaheim, California. 1955-60 saw them through a major expansion period. 1960-64 provided four Disney attractions for the 1964 New York World's Fair. 1965-71 saw the start of a project so monumental in private-sector development terms that many seasoned developers in America not known for their modesty indicated their scepticism in the feasibility of the Disney concept.

When the earth-moving equipment moved into Sections 2 and 11 on the map of Orange County, Florida, in mid-1967, the first tentative steps were taken in making the dream a reality. Four and a half years later Phase 1 of the Vacation Resort in Florida was opened. Eight thousand workers representing every type of building skill flooded the site. Prior to the removal of a single scoop of earth one primary standard had been established in connection with site clearance. That standard was

the retention of the natural beauty of the land. Most staggering of all the pieces of the puzzle that had to be linked together to accomplish Walt Disney World was the physical movement of 8,000,000 cubic yards of earth - perhaps the biggest earth-moving operation since the Hoover dam.

The purpose of this massive project was three-fold. It began with the engineering need to build up construction sites for the themepark and theme resort hotels. Second, the land was almost totally flat - both architectural and landscape designers sought to give these contours some variety; and third, almost as a bonus of the need for land fill, the Seven Seas Lagoon was created to achieve the water-oriented attraction Walt Disney foresaw on his early trips to the site.

One of the prime lessons designers, engineers and the day-to-day operating staff had learnt at Disneyland was the need for access to show areas day and night without interfering with 'the show'. To accomplish this meant going underground, providing basement access not only for personnel but for utilities and supplies. Because the prime construction sites were ready at water table level, creating underground corridors meant building up the site to a level of 14 ft in many areas of the themepark, rather than excavating.

Each morning, prior to the opening of the Magic Kingdom, as many as 6,000 people may be moving underground in a bustling world filled with utility conduits, warehousing and refrigerator facilities, employee wardrobes and service areas. Service vehicles deliver food and merchandise used by guests directly to the restaurants and commercial outlets within the Park.

The landscaping story began in 1967 when a 25-acre nursery was established on the northern edge of the site. If Walt Disney World was to be a world - with Asian jungles, European castles and Polynesian-style villages - then trees and shrubs indigenous to many areas of the globe were needed. The purpose of the nursery was, therefore, initially experimental: to discover what plant material not ordinarily native to central Florida could adapt.

Into this setting the foresters imported trees as young stock with origins as far away as New Zealand, Japan and Africa. A wide range was imported from California, Texas and other states. By opening day the landscapers had

planted nearly 60,000 trees and shrubs of 800 varieties. To create instant greenery for lawns, embankments and along roadways, enough turf was laid to cover 500 football fields. Thousands of trees were transplanted in new homes - the largest living oak for Liberty Square weighed fully 35 tons. It is interesting that Disney's commitment to set an example of good development in planning, use of space, water control, pollution prevention, building codes definition and conservation seems to have been achieved.

They have also introduced methods, which are crucial to major developments, for curtailing the intrusion of the building process. This is simply accomplished in separate developments great distances apart, but it is extremely difficult to achieve in more confined circumstances. The organisation that goes into transportation, movement of service and delivery vehicles, contract organisation and building compounds is exemplary. They have rediscovered the berm as a device for the containment of unsightly parking and maintenance areas. They have introduced the electrically operated vehicle for work in the undercroft. The movie's capability for improvisation provides temporary sets to allow additional attractions to be installed. Perhaps the most remarkable achievement is to pull together the greatest 'new town' maintenance unit in the world. A constant 'high' of good husbandry ensures that the shabby, the unkempt and the unclean never get an even chance to succeed.

Each day over 500 basic skill types constantly monitor and effectively maintain the most diverse and complex series of building artefacts. A typical day could include: replacement of character heads; repair of underwater foliage; repair to AM/FM radios; new locks; replacement signing; a new coat of paint on a park bench; fountain repair; sensor systems adjustments; modification of shade controls; adjustments to the iron rides; costume manufacture; laundering; Audio-Animatronic modification - and all this in addition to a park cleaning system which employs 300 people, steam-cleans the streets and polishes every floor and every sheet of glass daily before the first visitor arrives in the park.

Building 1.5 billion dollars of development at Walt Disney World, culminating in EPCOT '82, would be enough for most organisations. To build it to a level of daily usability and freshness is quite unique.

Land Pavilion

Community of Nations

Future World at EPCOT

Tomorrowland Construction

River Country

Monorail extension

Disney Landscape

The Empress

Tom Sawyer Island

New Orleans Square

Nature was inevitably the co-artist with Disney from the start in 1955 - Nature, that is, with a little assistance from Evans and Reeves Nurseries Inc. The speed of installation in Disneyland seems inconceivable. Plans were still being prepared in April and the park was opened in July of 1955. Walt Disney had wanted a green park - everything ever-green - for he recalled the cold winters of his child-hood in the east and opined that Disneyland must be eternal spring. He also wanted size in trees - the larger the better, so that the park would look cool and inviting. This was no small order for there are relatively few evergreen trees of a size which can be boxed successfully. A compromise was then found to include deciduous species for colour and contrast in foliage and texture - peach trees, crapemyrtles, jacaranda and coral trees.

Disneyland was a minnow in landscaping terms compared to WED's new challenge of landscaping some 2,500 acres of the 27,400 acres of Walt Disney World. A vast and imaginative land-use programme including water control and utility planning was launched in 1967 with the passage of special legislation by the State of Florida establishing the Reedy Creek Improvement District. The water control plan will ultimately include 55 miles of winding canals and 22 automatic float gates to maintain the level and flow of water, even under extreme rainfall conditions. A water-orientated attraction was carried a stage further when the site for the Magic Kingdom was isolated. An entire area unsuitable for construction because the land was low and wet could be turned into a major asset, they reasoned, by extending Bay Lake towards the west. By 1970, Seven Seas Lagoon was a reality, when the last concrete channel connecting it to Bay Lake was opened to water traffic. The man-made Seven Seas Lagoon was nearly a mile square, contained three islands, covered a water surface of 200 acres and sounded an average depth of 10 ft. The necessity of dealing with wet land stimulated not only a lagoon water attraction but also prime locations for the 'theme resort' hotels which connected and inter-related with the themepark. Running parallel to the macro-scale landscape planning was a major ecology programme whose impetus came from the Disney organisation. Initially 7,500 acres of cypress swampland was set aside as a conservation area, forming a refuge for rare plants and wildlife. The ecological surveys that followed determined the early conservation programme. The US Geological Survey (Department of the Interior) was contracted to coordinate a jointly financed seven-year study of the area's hydrology related to projected urbanisation.

The study called for the federal body to monitor waters outside the Disney property, while RCID and Disney scientists maintained constant testing of water quality inside the boundaries.

Three surveys, completed in 1975, prefaced invest-igations into new technologies and resulted in pioneering environmental systems at Walt Disney World. Action of the waters is monitored by a satellite in stationary orbit 23,000 miles above the equator. Employing electronic sensors and radio telemetry, measures the level, flow rate and chemistry of the Reedy Creek water to ensure maximum protection to the environment.

A modern waste-water treatment plant, constructed to treat sewage by the activated sludge process, uses bacteria and air to break down organic matter. Capable of routinely handling 3.3 million gallons of waste-water a day, the plant surpasses state standards for sewage treatment. To keep it well ahead of Walt Disney World's projected growth, the plant is being expanded to a 5-million gallons per day capacity.

One unusual aspect of the waste-water treatment system is a Living Filter Tree Farm. Here the treated effluent is used to spray-irrigate 148 acres of trees and shrubs. The natural growth processes of the vegetation remove the excess nutrients from the waste-water and return them to the water table in a recycled condition - an excellent testing ground for new plants for the Vacation Kingdom as well as being a sewage treatment system.

The newest experience at the plant is a prototype programme to use the water hyacinth as a waste-water purifier and as a new source of energy and agricultural soil conditioner. The project will demonstrate the use of the local weed as a tertiary filtration device for stripping nutrients from waste-water and then as a source of fuel and fertiliser.

In addition to waste-water treatment, researchers will concurrently investigate the practicality of harvesting the enriched hyacinth to produce useful by-products such as methane gas, fertiliser, ethyl alcohol and protein feedstock.

Despite the formidable scale of the total landscap-ing solution it is, I think, safe to say the picture most guests carry away from Disney World is of the incredible variety and tapestry of landscape found in the park. In each area landscape is an integral park of the scene, carefully planned and themed to the story.

The junge of Adventureland is, for example, really a series of mini-jungles, with each section authentic-ally representing vegetation from the tropical zone recreated. Delicate miniatures are cultivated for the fantasy setting of Disneyland storybook land, while nearby, full-size topiaries, each grown and shaped for five years, provide a whimsical backdrop for 'It's a Small World'. Tall pine forests create a wilderness for Frontier Land, while colourful floral gardens create a formal manicured setting for Main Street.

Altogether more than 2,000 different varieties of plant life are found throughout Disneyland and Walt Disney World, with more than 1½ million annuals changed each year, often to suit the mood of the season.

Sleeping Beauty Castle Disneyland

Walt

During Walt Disney's long career he frequently commented on his philosophy of life, his ideals, dreams and hopes of a better world. It is perhaps pertinent to an understanding of the Disney design philosophy to choose at random a selection of quotations drawn from speeches, interviews, film scripts and newspaper and magazine articles.

ART
'I don't pretend to know anything about art. I make pictures for entertainment, and then the professors tell me what they mean.'
'I am in no sense of the word a great artist, not even a great animator; I have always had men working for me whose skills were greater than my own. I am an idea man.'

AUDIENCES
'You can't live on things made for children - or for critics. I've never made films for either of them. Disneyland is not just for children. I don't play down.'

CHALLENGE
'It's kind of fun to do the impossible.'

CURIOSITY
'There is no secret about our approach. We keep things moving forward - opening up new doors and doing new things - because we're curious and curiosity keeps leading us down new paths. We're always exploring and experimenting. At WED, we call it Imagineering -the blending of creative imagination with technical know-how.'

COMMUNICATION
'All of us who use the implements of mass communications have a tremendous responsibility to utilise them more fully in the interest of common humanity in the light of present world conditions.'

DILIGENCE
'The way to get started is to quit talking and begin doing.'

DISNEYLAND
'Almost everyone warned us that Disneyland would be a Hollywood spectacular - a spectacular failure. But they were thinking about an amusement park, and we believed in our idea - a family park where parents and children could have fun - together.'
'I don't want the public to see the world they live in while they're in the Park. I want them to feel they're in another world.'
'It's something that will never be finished. Something that I can keep developing, keep plussing and adding to. It's alive. It will be a live, breathing thing that will need change. I wanted something alive, something that could grow, something I could keep plussing with ideas. Not only can I add things but even the trees will keep growing. The thing will get more beautiful each year. And as I find out what the public likes . . . I can change it, because it's alive.'

FUTURE
'The only problem with anything of tomorrow is that at the pace we're going right now, tomorrow would catch up with us before we got it built.'

GENIUS
'We allow no geniuses around our Studio.'

IDEAS
'I use the whole plant for ideas. If the janitor has a good idea, I'd use it.'

INNOVATION
'I believe in being an innovator.'

PERFECTION
'I'm not the perfectionist any more. It's my staff. They're the ones always insisting on doing something better and better. I'm the fellow trying to hurry them to finish before they spoil the job. You can overwork drawing or writing and lose the spontaneity.'

PERSONNEL
'You can dream, create, design and build the most wonderful place in the world . . . but it requires people to make the dream a reality.'

WALT DISNEY WORLD
'The one thing I learned from Disneyland was to control the environment. Without that we get blamed for the things that someone else does. When they come here they're coming because of an integrity that we've established over the years.'

WED ENTERPRISES
'Well, WED is, you might call it my backyard laboratory, my workshop away from work. It served a purpose in that some of the things I was planning, like Disneyland for example . . . it's pretty hard for banking minds to go with it . . . so I had to go ahead on my own and develop it to a point where they could begin to comprehend what I had on my mind.'

Facts

AREAS

Disneyland	76.6 acres
Disneyland Car Park	107.3 acres
Walt Disney World	27,433 acres
Magic Kingdom WDW	100 acres
EPCOT Center	600 acres
Wildlife Conservation area	7,500 acres
Vacation Kingdom	3,000 acres

The area of Walt Disney World is equivalent to the area of San Francisco or twice the size of Manhattan Island.

ATTENDANCE

Disneyland since 1955 has received 210,000,000 guests. Walt Disney World since 1971 has received 126,000,000 guests.
Current annual attendance is between 13 and 14 million visitors.
1 in 4 Florida visitors goes to Walt Disney World.
Single Peak Day attendances — December 31st 1980, WDW 92,969 guests.
Guests to Walt Disney World spent $14 billion in first ten years - 3½ times the forecast figure.
At Walt Disney World guests bought enough Mickey Mouse caps to supply the population of Chicago, and enough Mickey Mouse Tee Shirts to clothe the population of Australia.
Adult Disney guests outnumbered children 3:1.

EMPLOYMENT

Disneyland employs between 5,000 low season and 8,000 high season, Walt Disney World between 12,000 low season and 15,000 high season. Walt Disney World ten-year payroll totalled $952,000,000. Disneyland hosts use 5,500 costumes daily, 325 types and 450,000 articles.

EXPANSION

Disneyland original 17 attractions, currently 57.
Walt Disney World original 35 attractions, currently 45.
Lodging before Disneyland opened 5 hotels plus 2 motels in Anaheim, providing 87 rooms plus 34 restaurants.
Currently 130 hotels and motels providing 12,000 rooms, plus 400 restaurants.
Walt Disney World offered Disney the opportunity to provide Disney standard hotels, 3,500 rooms in the first phase, 825 camp ground sites and 400 vacation villas, plus 3 further hotel sites allocated. Within one year of WDW opening major American chains had planned to provide 11,759 rooms in the Orlando area.

FOOD

Disneyland: 60,000 meals served daily with food centres in the Park serving 4,000 people per hour.
Walt Disney World: Since opening more than 250,000 meals have been served.
All food for the Magic Kingdom is processed and portioned at the Central Food Facility and distributed to the finishing kitchens via eight acres of underground service routes and basements.
During the first full year of operation at Walt Disney World in 1972, average daily consumption included:
7,000 lb hamburgers
14,547 individual servings
15,000 sandwiches
2,280 gallons sauces and dressings
1,250 cases of lettuce
3,715 dozen cakes, pastries and rolls.

INVESTMENT

Disneyland costs by opening day 1955: $17,000,000. Current investment: $212,000,000. Walt Disney World expenditure by opening day 1971: $400,000,000. Current investment: $700,000,000. Estimated when EPCOT Center opens October 1982 - total investment in Walt Disney World will be $1.5 billion.

LANDSCAPE

At Disneyland 500,000 trees, plants and shrubs are used in the landscape. At Walt Disney World 7,000,000 flowering plants were planted in the first ten years.

TRANSPORTATION

Monorail at Disneyland:
70,000,000 passengers have travelled over 1.75 million miles since 1959. At WDW the monorail travels 500,000 miles annually.
Parking facilities: There are parking facilities for 11,500 cars at Disneyland and 12,000 at Walt Disney World, in addition to a Disney Car Care Center.
Disney has the fifth largest fleet of passenger-carrying water craft in the world - over 400 boats and submarines.
Theme Park Transport:
Locomotives at Walt Disney World date from 1916 to 1925 to 1928. They run on 1½ miles of narrow-gauge track. In addition horse-drawn streetcars, horseless carriage omnibus, people movers and aerial cable cars are available in Disneyland and Walt Disney World.

Disney Landscape

EPCOT Landscaping

Cinderella Castle WDW

Contemporary Resort Area

Approach to WDW

Magic Kingdom Entrance WDW

Water Chute Resort Area

Polynesian Resort

Cinderella Castle WDW

Water Hyacinths

Greenhouse Hydroponics

Greenhouse

Topiary

Zero Gravity Lettuce Drum

Hydroponics

The Crystal Palace WDW

Disneyland Detail

The Metaphysical Themepark

Themeparks, and 'themed' buildings generally, have been recurrently intruding into architectural conversations since the sixties. Architects and critics who make such references have diverse reasons for doing so. For example, Peter Blake, in his *Form Follows Fiasco: Why Modern Architecture Hasn't Worked*, uses Disney World as a recriminating stick with which to beat the dead horse of Modernism. **'Some 50 years after Corbusier's first sketch for a Ville Radieuse, the most interesting new town built in the US in this century was completed in a swamp some 30 miles south of Orlando, Florida.'** Against the manifest failure of CIAM urban theory and practice, Blake implies, only Walt Disney delivers what people really want: pedestrian scale and streetscapes, old-fashioned yet newly and totally *planned*, smoothly serviced by the highest technologies, cleaner and safer than cities-as-we-know-them.

In 'You Have to Pay for the Public Life', Charles Moore thoughtfully draws the conclusion contained in the title: the diffused forces of contemporary urban culture have not, especially in southern California, created a public realm - except in the commercially contrived precincts of Disneyland. **'Curiously, for a public place, Disneyland is not free,'** allows Moore. **'You buy tickets at the gate. But then, Versailles cost someone a great deal of money too.'** Consequently this themepark, as a coin-operated urban model, **'must be regarded as the most important single construction in the West in the past several decades.'** Now by this time, 1965, Tom Wolfe had already 'discovered' Las Vegas (and compared it, too, to a proletarian Versailles), but Moore was among the first architects to explore themepark territory. Moore's essay does not, however, invoke popular culture as a validation of Disneyland. Instead, more like Peter Blake, he finds there and only there a traditional sense of **'place, indeed a whole public world, full of sequential occurrences . . . hierarchies'**, as in Old World townscapes. For the same reason in the same essay Moore extols the stage-set city of Santa Barbara, California, rebuilt after an earthquake in 1925 on a unified theme of 'movieland Spanish' architecture, yet possessed of arcades, patios and other public spaces. Unlike Blake, Moore could reconcile this atmospheric artifice with Modernism (or turn it into Post-Modernism), and it is tempting to believe he later applied the lessons of Disneyland and Santa Barbara to his own work, such as his Piazza d'Italia, New Orleans, 1976-79, themed in jokey Classical Orders.

It was Robert Venturi's overt aim in *Learning from Las Vegas* - the first published notes for which date from 1968 - to transmit to architects the lessons of commercial vernacular, just as high-style architecture had been enlivened before by the industrial vernacular of grain elevators, ships, bridges and factories, or the primitive vernacular exalted in *Architecture Without Architects*. The Las Vegas Strip which Venturi took as his field study was only common or ordinary strip-development raised to a higher power; he still focused on Roadtown's demonstrative self-advertising imagery.

When Venturi adopts it, practising what he preaches, into his firm's designs, something is changed in translation. It seemingly panders to popular iconography but can also be appreciated by sophisticated auditors of Post-Modernism for the wit, irony and ambiguity of that knowing indulgence. Conversely, a 'genuine' thematic symbol system is never deliberately double-coded, complex or contradictory. (A duck-shaped building sells ducks.) Indeed, much of its attraction resides in the directness of an *architecture parlante* such as

Modernism forfeited when it expunged social ideology (and even that could be symbolically recondite enough) in favour of abstract aesthetics. Themepark architecture can be stylistically heterogeneous, impure or fraudulent, but its loaded content is always obvious. Because themeparks are devised as profit-making enterprises, their image-marketing *begins* with calculated audience appeal, explaining both their public popularity and the envy in which architects hold them. In addition to their simplistic working symbolism, themeparks often command an enviable standard of technology that really works, is unobtrusive if not invisible, and never *symbolic* (of a Machine Aesthetic or twentieth-century *Zeitgeist*). The rub is that architects, as such, remain peripheral to themepark planning, governed as it is by Disneyesque 'imagineering', environmental conditioning, software, set-design, landscaping and other expertise.

The publications of Venturi's research team at first provoked considerable hostility from critics alarmed at this apparent celebration of stylistic vulgarity, down-market banality and commercial disorder. Times have grown more tolerant, though, with the courting of Pop culture, 'radical chic' inversions of taste, and the critical transmutation of mass media from kitsch into Camp; hence by 1977 it seemed unexceptional, even obligatory, for Charles Jencks' *Language of Post-Modern Architecture* to credit both Las Vegas and Disneyland. In addition Jencks, in an article of 1975, had remarked on the kind of dissimulating, illusionistic construction requisite to themeparks, illustrating a building - prematurely aged with the *ersatz* ruination of instant history - at Knott's Berry Farm, Los Angeles, an immediate precursor of Disneyland.

ALL-AMERICAN HEAVEN . . .

Walt Disney no more invented the great American themepark than he invented the animated cartoon, but he did rationalise its technological, managerial and experiential dimensions into an unprecedented consummation. He had, since the early thirties, toyed with the notion of a small amusement park as a sideline; his vision burgeoned into an 'atmospheric' park of 185 acres. By the time it opened in 1955, Disney Productions had diversified into live-action features and television, thus its illusionistic acumen derived from his film studios in particular and the proximity of the Hollywood screen industry in general. (Universal Studios now runs a themepark based on movie-making itself.) Disney was in the fantasy business himself, unlike Walter and Cordelia Knott whose earlier park began in the twenties as a diversionary lure to sell the produce of Knott's Berry Farm to passers-by. **'Hollywood brought'**, as Reyner Banham put it, **'technical skill and resources in converting fantastic ideas into physical realities.'**

Banham also points out that a common denominator of Disneyland's design - a virtual theme in itself - is transportation, as appropriate to a southern Californian mentality obsessed with personal mobility. One can get around Disneyland by almost any mode of travel *except* driving one's own car: steam train, monorail, overhead cable Skyway, patented People Mover, submarines, canoes, rafts, paddle-steamer, sailing ship (sailing, that is, on tracks laid under the water), and jungle-cruise boats modelled, perhaps, on *The African Queen*. Fairground rides for their own sake include roller-coasters, bobsleds, 'rocket jets', spinning teacups and flying Dumbo elephants. Under-age drivers rehearse on a miniature freeway for kiddie cars. Main Street USA offers vintage vehicles of its period style, 1910: horse tram, fire engine, double-decker omnibus and motor carriages.

Main Street USA is also the main street of the park. It is entered past the train station, signboarded 'Disneyland, population 192,000,000' - that figure being the head-count of the whole United States, for here is its spiritual capital. All visitors must pass along Main Street which, it has been suggested by Disney's daughter among others, replicates the small Missouri town near Walt's boyhood farm; he would have been nine years old in 1910. The town's gracious, gaslit lifestyle was never enjoyed by his impoverished family - no playtime for hardworking little Walt - so a compensatory, picturesque idealisation rendered it for him, as for visitors to Disney's land, quainter, cleaner, simpler and altogether nicer than the real settings of real childhoods - or of today's real towns. Richard Schickel writes in his excellent biography of Disney: **'Disneyland, to him, was a living monument to himself and his ideas of what constituted the good, true and beautiful in this world. It was a projection, on a gigantic scale, of his personality . . . in the way that the pleasant grounds of Versailles were an extension of the Sun King.'** Disney freely admitted he meant his dream park not for children or anyone else, but his own gratification, and if it affected others similarly that was because they shared the same small-town and middle-class Midwestern ethos, its imagined backgrounds and lost memories displaced in California or wherever.

While on the one hand a personal Never Never Land, it is on the other hand a scientifically construed quantification of manipulated sentiment, an immaculate conception in its legendary cleanliness, staffed by youthful attendants with lockjaw smiles, its vistas designed to be photographed against guaranteed Kodachrome sunsets (the park lends free Instamatics and Polaroids). The vaunted 'human scale' of Main Street, admired by Peter Blake and Charles Moore, is a subtle illusion, everything, every brick, 5/8ths true size at ground-floor level, then diminishing proportionally upwards even more, imperceptibly. **'The whole thing is a marvel of technology applied to mass psychology . . . one of the most intelligently conceived pieces of architecture in America . . .'**

Anatomising the dream factory, Main Street leads to the Central Plaza, around which the circular park is divided into quadrants corresponding to sub-themes: Adventureland, Frontierland, Fantasyland and Tomorrowland. Frontierland, like Main Street, evokes nostalgia for a vital, innocent America that never was. Its Hollywood-style realism yields objective correlatives for the frontier myth, yet American architecture has been conjuring with the same theme ever since Frank Lloyd Wright's Prairie Houses (built just *after* the closure of the frontier and rarely on prairies); latterly these symbolic homesteads were debased into suburban 'ranches'. Knott's Berry Farm had prefigured Disney too; there a ghost town resurrected the pioneer spirit, a steam train conveyed visitors through a phoney desert (where phoney train robbers lurked), and the paddle-steamer *Cordelia K* made its maiden voyage long before Frontierland's *Mark Twain*.

The past (sometimes confused with 'history') is more fictive than the future here. Diametrically opposite Frontierland, in plan, is Tomorrowland. The latter is not themed on science fiction (literature belongs in Fantasyland) but on a blandly factual future graphed from today into literal tomorrow, or the day after. The simulated Flight to Mars is convincingly familiar already from NASA's Mission Control. The robots are real (or the humans are artificial - all how you look at it, despite the shock of recognition that the actors in Disneyland's Mission Control are Audio-Animatronic mechanicals). On the Submarine Voyage the vessels are scaled-down from the US Navy's nuclear-powered Polaris-missile class. The mandatory, perennial monorail has been **'the transportation system of tomorrow'** (quote, Disneyland guidebook) for as long as anyone can remember. This is the stuff of the World's Fairs that, throughout the twentieth century, have amounted to themeparks predicated on a perfectible near-future of Scientific Progress. Abiding faith in Better Living Through Electricity is particularly American, representing one magnetic pole of the national dream machine, the other - by no means mutually exclusive - being the cultural anachronism of Main Street 1910 or Frontierland. The present (sometimes confused with 'reality') gets left out in the unrepresented middle.

When James Rouse, developer of the new town of Columbia, Maryland, says **'The greatest piece of urban design in the US today is Disneyland,'** he seems to be adducing it as a *practical* planning paradigm *for* today. If so, it is hardly urban by Los Angeles standards. Nonetheless, in 1966 Disney himself publicly declared his intense interest in city planning, stemming from dismay at the messy sprawl of Los Angeles. He subsequently turned his attention to Disney World, for which he had purchased in 1964 a 27,500-acre virgin Florida tract, twice the size of Manhattan Island. His second Magic Kingdom was completed in 1971 (posthumously - Disney had died late in 1966). True, the core of the new park is even smaller than Disneyland, while exactly duplicating most of its fixtures: Main Street USA, Sleeping Beauty's Castle, the same four quadrants around a Central Plaza, and so on. The rest has been developed as an Experimental Prototype Community of Tomorrow, EPCOT, due to be inaugurated in October 1982. Entirely man-made under private enterprise, this colony of 20,000 inhabitants will house Disney World's employees, visiting tourists and resident scientists whose experiments-in-progress occupy World Fair's structures ranging from an eighteen-storey geodesic sphere to underwater laboratories. Tomorrowland has arrived, but EPCOT also recapitulates the history and architecture of cities through such tokens as an oriental pagoda, a Moroccan minaret, a reduced Eiffel Tower, Les Halles market (the reproduction is now more 'real' than the demolished Paris original), and that favourite of urbanists, Venice's Piazza San Marco. All the world's a themepark, and we are but Audio-Animatronic robots in it.

... AND HELL

Disneyland's idealised Americana is less apt as a simile for Utopia (since it ignores social relations) than for Heaven. Because its illusionism transcends America's 'real' physical environment too, it amounts to a *meta*physical construct. And if Disneyland projects a sanitised, mythical earthly paradise or Heaven, observers have noted, then America's complementary fun-house version of Hell must be Las Vegas. To pursue this metaphysical symmetry - for the one demands the other - is to expand the scope of 'themeparks', yet the present survey is after all more concerned with architectural theming than with proprietary amusement parks. Although unbounded by a simple perimeter with turnstiles separating the world of illusion from the carparks, still Las Vegas is so coherent in its urban design language that it has inspired the most thorough study of theming to date, *Learning from Las Vegas* by Venturi *et al.* **'Las Vegas is analyzed here only as a phenomenon of architectural communication,'** avows Venturi; **'its values are not questioned.'** Whereas he there-

fore deals with its *means* rather than *meanings*, Las Vegas is thematically all about Sin, or at least guilty fun. If not diabolically wicked, the immorality on offer contravenes the Protestant Ethic to which subscribe most of those who descend - for the purpose - unto Sin City. Tom Wolfe maintains **'Las Vegas is a resort for old people,'** predominantly, hell-bent on defying - for the duration - small-town and middle-class taboos against drinking, gambling, girlie shows and **'staying out late'**. My own intuition is that hardworking Americans holiday there expressly to throw away money - either as a propitiary sacrifice or to show liberating contempt for that which holds them in thrall the rest of the year - with a cathartic abandon made painless by the pretext of 'games of chance'.

Hell is of course more colourful than Heaven (as Dante and Milton confirm), but the commercialised vice of Las Vegas, far from anarchic, is as well-regulated as Disneyland. Gambling, prostitution and quickie divorce are legal, or at any rate not illegal, run by the State (through licences) and private enterprise much to their profit like any other businesses (there aren't many), while much of this adult playground is owned lock, stock and shotgun-barrel by *organised* crime, the Syndicate.

Besides its lenient laws the State of Nevada provides a unique geographical context. Seventh largest State in the Union, its population density is 1/44th of the national average. The major concentration, Las Vegas, is within dirty-weekend range of Los Angeles (City of the Angels) and the minor one, Reno, within striking distance of San Francisco (City of St Francis), so the two vice-and-dice centres beckon, like Sodom and Gomorrah, just over the border from California, most populous of all the States. However, Sin City is necessarily *insulated* from the neighbourhood of decent folks by sterile wastelands so worthless that their other main use has been as testing grounds for atomic weapons. Las Vegas' Spanish name, meaning 'fertile plains', is misleading (like Greenland); there was precious little water before construction of the Hoover Dam. In today's local landscape, the green of nature betrays the cultivating hand of man (but beware of imitations: Astroturf or green gravel lawns). Between Las Vegas and the southern Californian catchment area of its clientele, linked by the *cordon sanitaire* of Route 91, lies the Mojave Desert, with Death Valley nearby.

Given the region's arid climate (no weather, no seasons, just unchanging climate) of daily cerulean skies and slow-baking heat, these natural constants can be superseded by internal environmental controls: air-conditioning and 'mood' lighting. Venturi describes how casino interiors are kept low for air-conditioning efficiency, closed to external views and very dark with pools of light over the gaming tables. Light never defines spatial boundaries. Sometimes ceilings are mirrored, not only for security surveillance through one-way glass but to further deny architectonic spatiality. The ambiguous, limitless spaces evince contemporary indifference to the traditional aesthetic of monumental communal spaces, according to Venturi, and the (intended) psychological effect is of round-the-clock disorientation.

That artificial microcosm, typical of themeparks, is expedited by Las Vegas' island-like isolation. Add all other ambient inputs to this unremitting sound-and-light show at full intensity, and it can be dangerous to get out of synch with it. Hunter Thompson in his classic of manic dementia, *Fear and Loathing in Las Vegas*, attempts escape by infusions of consciousness-altering chemicals and concludes, **'No, this is not a good town for**

psychedelic drugs. **Reality itself is too twisted.'** Thompson's infernal, subjective account should be read as a cautionary foil to those by Wolfe and Venturi, who report from outside the total illusion. As Marlow's Mephistopheles reminds us: **'Why, this is Hell, nor am I out of it.'**

Night does make a difference to the Las Vegas skyline, for then the buildings disappear to be replaced with what Wolfe calls the 'electrographic architecture' of signs. Venturi is more interested in the way these super-signs function, communicating messages (and luring customers) via large-scale, legible symbolism of a sort historical architecture once had and which Modernism, to the great regret of Venturi *et al*, has lost. On the Las Vegas strip **'the sign is more important than the architecture'**; certainly signs, such as the twenty-two-storey neon landmark advertising the Dunes Hotel, dominate buildings; sometimes the buildings *are* signs, like the pulsating jukebox facades of Fremont Street. Tom Wolfe for his part treats the signs as pure style and seeks its origins among the designers of those light displays. None of them trained at **'the design schools of Eastern universities'**, although one, he finds, had been an artist for Walt Disney. But exactly!

The architectural house style of Las Vegas's hotels and casinos can be traced more directly to the Flamingo, built in 1945. To say Bugsy Siegel was to Las Vegas as Walt Disney was to the Magic Kingdom would hardly be fair to the memory of either party, albeit both founded service industries for the post-war Leisure Society. In fact Siegel's Flamingo Hotel-Casino set the theme for Las Vegas a full decade earlier than Disneyland. From Florida coastal resorts the Flamingo imported its name and a stylistic idiom aptly identified by Venturi as a corrupt International Modernism derived from Corbusier by way of Brazil. To Las Vegas - a new Miami Beach without the beach - the Flamingo bequeathed its *leitmotif* of 'free forms' or, as Wolfe particularises it: **'Boomerang Modern supports, Palette Curvilinear bars, Hot Shoppe Cantilever roofs, and a scalloped swimming pool'**. A taste for such shapes has not only been parlayed into countless motels, service stations, hamburger stands *etc*, lining every American roadside strip, but still informs Las Vegas architecture, even if more eclectic mixes - *eg* the half-timbered Aladdin or the cod classicism of Caesar's Palace - have been added to the generic theme.

Thus Wolfe asserts with typical hyperbole that **'Overnight the Baroque Modern forms made Las Vegas one of the few architecturally unified cities in the world,'** and again, **'Las Vegas and Versailles are the only two architecturally uniform cities in Western history.'** Robert Venturi sees the layout of parking lots as analogous to the landscape planning of Versailles (**'grids of lampposts substitute for obelisks and rows of urns and statues, as points of identity and continuity in the vast space'**), and likens Las Vegas to Rome as well (sequences of **'churches in the religious capital, casinos and their signs in the entertainment capital'**). Professional architects, though, were not so much image-makers themselves as instruments of the grand theming dictated by, say, Bugsy Siegel. Furthermore, architects' responsibility is limited to facades; otherwise Las Vegas casinos consist of shed-like enclosures, their visual impact given by signs in front or above - designed by specialists - and their environmental control by engineers, planting mechanical equipment on the flat roofs or in the back. The remaining design act is relegated to gridding off so many square feet inside to be glamourised by interior decorators.

imagineering

The WED and MAPO team of 'Imagineers' includes hundreds
of artists, designers, architects, writers, engineers and others
with a variety of special skills. This creative team is responsible for
the creation of all shows, attractions and outdoor entertainment
for Disneyland, Walt Disney World, Epcot Center and
Tokyo Disneyland.

Founded by Walt Disney in 1952, WED's first assignment
was the master-planning and design of Disneyland.
Following this was the creation of four major shows for the 1964
New York World's Fair and, of course, the opening of
Walt Disney World in 1971.

Today, the WED and MAPO 'Imagineers' are devoting their
entire effort to the creation and design of Epcot Center
and Tokyo Disneyland. Using Epcot Center's 'World of Motion'
show as an example, the Disney creative process has been
highlighted for you here and in the various areas throughout
the WED and MAPO facilities.

STORYBOARD: The storyboard enables artists and writers to visually organise the initial sequences of scenes.

SCRIPT: The scriptwriter contributes the storyline, narration and dialogue to the show's conceptual development.

CONCEPT: The initial concepts for the show are formulated by the Show Designer.

SHOW MODELS: From set designs and storyboards, Model Builders construct miniatures of the various show scenes.

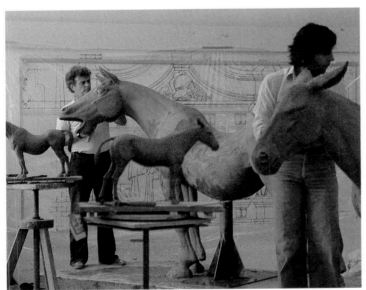

SCULPTURE: Audio-Animatronic figures are sculptured, first in miniature, then full size.

SHOW SET DESIGN: Designers take the concept from storyboard and scale models to actual set designs and blueprints.

GRAPHICS: All show graphics and signing are individually designed.

INTERIORS: Here the many fixtures and props for the show are selected.

ARCHITECTURAL DESIGN: Working with the show set designers, architects design the physical structure in which the show is presented.

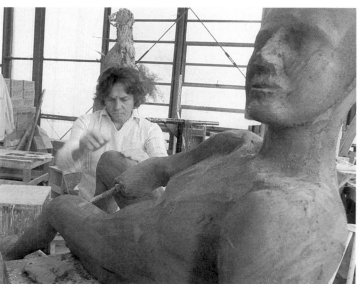

MOULDS and CASTING: At MAPO several plaster moulds are made of clay figures. From these a fibreglass shell is cast and covered with flexible 'skin'.

WARDROBE and FIGURE FINISHING: From MAPO, figures are sent back to WED for fur, feathers, paint and wigs. Wardrobe designs are furnished by Disneyland.

ELECTRONIC/MECHANICAL DESIGN/MANUFACTURE: At MAPO fibreglass shells encase the electronic/mechanical workings of the Audio-Animatronic figures.

SHOW SETS and PROP CONSTRUCTION: Full-sized show sets are constructed from smaller models at the Tujunga facility.

SHOW SETS and PROP CONSTRUCTION: Unique, one-of-a-kind props are also individually fabricated.

ANIMATION: This console and computer help programme the life-like movements of the show's Audio-Animatronic figures.

AUDIO: Final show tracks including sound effects, dialogue, narration and music score are mixed here.

SPECIAL EFFECTS and LIGHTING: The mood and atmosphere are enhanced by the special effects and lighting created by WED 'illusioneering' laboratory.

CONSTRUCTION: takes shape on the EPCOT Center Construction site.

Disney Detail

Detail with Disney starts with people. Not just the 8,000 cast members in the park or the 500 different support skills that provide the park maintenance groups, but the inbuilt detail that streams out of the WED and MAPO. WED Enterprises is the Imagineering branch of the Disney organisation responsible for the master-planning, design, engineering and creation of all the attractions for the four major projects; Disneyland, Walt Disney World, Tokyo Disneyland and EPCOT. MAPO brings to life the design of the WED engineers; Audio-Animatronic figures, ride vehicles, control systems and a variety of 'one of a kind' creations are fabricated at MAPO, the prototype research development and manufacturing branch of Walt Disney Productions.

In the final analysis everyone involved views the design of the theme as a complete unit in which all elements, major and minor, work together in a harmonious relationship. This means keeping contradictions to an absolute minimum. Contradictions in the Disney vernacular specifically refer to conflicting elements - to factors which appear out of place to the eye or ear or other senses. A popcorn box in a flower bed . . . blue grass banjo music in Adventureland - these and other similar contradictions can be controlled in the day-to-

Telephone Scene

Islamic Knowledge

China EPCOT

day operations, but the possibilities of thematic contradictions, visually conflicting structures and other major elements are scrupulously avoided. This is done with a kind of unique overkill. Altogether there are more than 45,000 individual signs at Disneyland and Disney World. They range from hand-lettered price cards to complex attraction graphics. Weeks may be invested in the design and production of a single sign, the style and typeface carefully chosen to enhance the architecture. Themed drinking fountains and cash registers can be seen in many areas. Even the trash cans are hand-painted to blend in with the immediate environment. Faithfully maintained, these designs require more than 20,000 different colours and all have been catalogued and stored in Disney paint shops. Disney entertainment is often communication without words, an international communication that is understood by Americans and foreign visitors alike. Much of it is visual in nature - sometimes very evident, sometimes subtle, but always a skilful orchestration of colours, lighting, special effects, motion and shapes.

Part of the Disney success is the ability to create a believable world of dreams that appeals to every member of the family. The detail is the language that makes this possible.

Italy Model: EPCOT

Minnie

Signing

People Mover

Computer Controls

Tom Sawyer Island Bridge

Cultivation

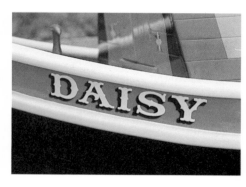

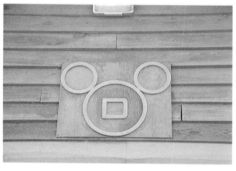

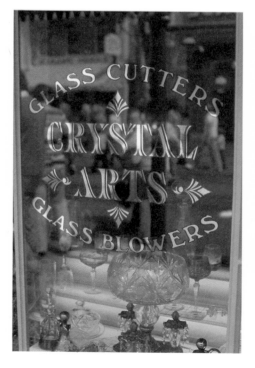

The Disneyland News

EDWARD T. MECK

EDITOR IN CHIEF

CLOSED

Entrance

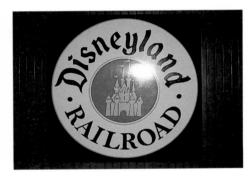

Disneyland RAILROAD

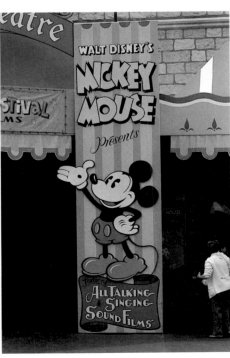

theatre

WALT DISNEY'S MICKEY MOUSE Presents

FESTIVAL FILMS

ALL TALKING SINGING SOUND FILMS

U.S. POSTAGE STAMPS

Disney Transportation

Steamboatin'

Fort Wilderness Railroad

Jungle Cruise

Reading the matrix of 'How to get where you are going in Walt Disney World' gives some indication of the total transportation plan available for the visitor. Green, red, blue, red, white and gold-flagged buses, monorail, Magic Kingdom ferry and watercraft provide the external links. Inside the Magic Kingdom the WEDway People Mover, the sky buckets and steam trains augment these, together with the many other transportation modes available in the rides themselves - horseless carriages, steamboats, jungle launches, submarines and a multiplicity of railed conveyors.

Since the early days of Disneyland, Walt Disney had wanted to include the train of the future. After much research and study WED engineers returned from Germany much impressed by the experimental monorail developed by the Altweg company. After recommending the system Disney designers joined with the Altweg staff in 1958 to develop a basic plan leading to a working prototype and the Disneyland monorail became the first passenger-carrying system of its kind in the Western hemisphere.

At present ten trains and five local trains with a capacity of 200 passengers, and five express trains with a 240-passenger capacity make up the Vacation Kingdom monorail system. The Walt Disney World Mark IV monorail trains are 171 ft long (express trains are 201 ft) and are wider than their Disneyland counterparts, incorporating a new air suspension system for the smoothest possible ride. The trains are engineered to attain speeds up to 45 miles per hour but the system is capable of much higher speeds in other uses. All vehicles are climate-controlled and passengers may enter on either side of the train.

The system at Walt Disney World provides two concrete beamways side by side over a three-mile circuit, plus another 3,000 ft of single beamway to connect with maintenance yards.

Carrying 10,000 passengers an hour, the system encircles the 300-acre Seven Seas Lagoon in the heart of the Vacation area. Guests may travel by monorail from the parking area and the transportation centre to the Magic Kingdom or to the theme hotels nearby.

The noiseless, all-electric trains travel some 64 ft above ground level. At one point the twin beams cross a ship channel joining Bay Lake and the Seven Seas Lagoon, then pass directly through the heart of the Contemporary Resort Hotel at the fourth-floor concourse level.

For the eight-mile extension of the monorail system for EPCOT 400 beams and 325 piers have been cast on site - a special casting process has been developed for the 65-ton pre-stressed steel reinforced beams. They are formed around a styrofoam core to produce a super-strength but lightweight concrete rail.

With more than 400 ships and boats carrying 10,000,000 guests annually, Walt Disney World ranks as the fifth largest passenger carrying fleet in the world. Submarines, side-wheeler steamboats, island ferries and colourful sailboats carry guests to all parts of the Magic Kingdom resort hotels and recreation areas. The biggest ships in the fleet are two 600-passenger ferryboats carrying guests to the main entrance of the Magic Kingdom.

Four steam locomotives also operate in Walt Disney World using a standard 36-inch narrow gauge track which runs one and a half miles around the periphery of the Magic Kingdom. The locomotives were originally built in Philadelphia between 1916 and 1928. They were purchased in 1969 in Mexico and were completely rebuilt in a Tampa shipyard over a two-year period. The locomotives operate on a steam pressure of 150 lb between 10 and 12 miles per hour. They are diesel-fuelled and weigh approximately 35 tons.

Perhaps the great innovation in transportation terms by Disney is the WEDway People Mover transit system - which has now been installed commercially at Houston Airport. The main advantage of the system is its lack of gear belts or other mechanical devices. The wheels and doors are the only moving points in the entire system. A series of pollution-free linear induction motors embedded in the track creates a magnetic field that pushes the five three-car trains along 7,200 ft of track at up to 15 miles per hour. The operation of the system is controlled and monitored by a mini-computer. In actual operation at Walt Disney World the WEDway People Mover has performed at 99.8% per cent efficiency Energy conservation is another feature of the system. Sensors along the People Mover route ensure that power is applied only to linear induction motors which are directly under a train. The average cost of operating the People Mover is 9 cents a passenger mile. Contributing to the system's safety record is the block zone behind each vehicle which prevents power from being supplied to motors in that zone and ensures that safe distances are maintained between trains. In addition there is no exposed power rail. This fascination for a combination of restoration and innovation is the hallmark of all the Disney thinking. The use of self-induced paradox is as necessary to the designers in transportation as it is in the design of sets of the Magic Kingdom. What is equally fascinating is the creation of a maintenance section that can deal with all the problems posed by this variety of transportation modes, and perhaps even more significant than this versatility is the bottom line to all operators - reliability in use. WEDway leads the way, but all the other transportation methods score very close to full marks. London Transport please note.

Transportation Main Street

People Mover: Disneyland

Disneyworld Station

WEDway People Mover

WDW Truck

WDW Main Street

Steam train + Monorail WDW

WDW Monorail

WDW Monorail

WDW Monorail

Car Park WDW

Derek Walker
Architecture and Themeing

Walt and Mickey

Until Disneyland was developed in 1955 there was no 'themepark' product in the United States. At that time financial institutions in the entertainment world were fairly unanimous in their consensus that the concept could not generate sufficient income to give a satisfactory return on the large capital investment required.

Disneyland was the pioneer which educated the financier and consumer, enabling subsequent themeparks to enter the marketplace with public acceptance of the product already established.

Although it is imperative to recognise the extraordinary advantage which contributed to Disneyland's success as a pioneer product - the reservoir of characters, family image, links with the media and above all the flair and innovation shown in movies over 25 years, it is still difficult for the architectural profession to concede that Disney's first design exercise on the total environment showed a greater understanding of human aspirations and behavioural patterns than most city planners generate in a lifetime of urban activity.

When Peter Blake commented in *New York* magazine that **'The truth of the matter is the only new towns of any significance built in America since World War II are Disneyland in Anaheim, California and Disney World in Orlando, Florida. Both are "new", both are "towns" and both are staggeringly successful,'** he could have spoken for

the English New Towns movement too. Granted, Disney had, together with the power of personal conviction, a Medici-like control on the design and money buttons. He didn't have a mandate to produce a low-cost housing programme or medical, educational and welfare support systems. The uncanny instinct he did possess for autocratic environmental control could, if EPCOT had moved closer to the original concept as the Experimental Prototype Community Of Tomorrow, have passed down some useful lessons in the search for the 'City Beautiful'. It is possible that the non-democratic system with a profound insight into human needs and requirements could have proved a more interesting alternative to the bureaucratic labyrinth that produces complex urban living cells which represent such a watered-down compromise for today's society.

For more than two decades now people have asked 'Just what makes Disney so popular?' Each year more people visit Disneyland and Walt Disney World than all the professional football and basketball games combined. To be sure Disney's success is not due to a chance meeting of luck and spontaneity, but to a carefully orchestrated show that is indeed engineered and designed by motion picture people . . . It is a show that began in miniature form in Glendale at WED Enterprises. Everything is created through a form of storytelling, each attraction presenting an orderly set of scenes from the very beginning.

The imagineering format has been described earlier, but it is pertinent to stress the vital need for the three-dimensional approach as the Disney theme audience is placed right in the middle of the scene -thus the modelling process takes many forms and scales from paper cut-outs to full-size mock-ups.

The Disney planning formula, however, remains the same in Disneyland, Tokyo Disneyland and Disney World. The system of crowd flow is very simple. Main Street is an entrance corridor absorbing large masses of visitors in a short period of time. The guests move down the street to find a large hub from which the other lands or scenes radiate, like the spokes in a wheel. Each land featuring a visual centrepiece is easy to enter and leave because all paths lead back to the central hub. Though Disney World is based on a looser scale than its Californian parent, the plan form is identical. Streets are wider, both to carry more people and because computer analysis indicated that its more complex layout would make visitors pause at diverging points and therefore consume more space. Wider streets in turn dictated taller buildings. Even so, one could not accuse Disney World of monumentalism.

Main Street is still only 55 ft wide and the Town Square only 200 x 145 ft. It is perhaps in this manipulation of tight space, born out of Hollywood and studio illusion, that the Disney designers excel. They are adept at the use of 'forced perspective' which makes buildings and other objects appear

taller and further away. Through this process the buildings and landscaping are scaled progressively smaller towards the rear or top of a scene. The result to the eye is the illusion of a dramatically larger and deeper scene than actually exists. This process, coupled with the obsessive detailing unnoticed by most guests, produces the visual experience which is the true art of the Disney theme.

In a world of increasing architectural eclecticism Disney World and Las Vegas between them offer the 'Acropolis equivalent'. Disney's formula is manifestly more successful in the aura of a rose-coloured definition of the past: New Orleans without the squalor, Frontierland without the blood. It is only when Disney turns towards the future that the inconsistencies start to emerge. The architecture seems to be wholly inhibited by Walt Disney's own scepticism about anticipation.

'The only problem of anything of tomorrow is that at the pace we are going right now tomorrow would catch up with us before we got it built.' In a sense this has happened in Tomorrowland and this area of the Magic Kingdom suffers from a real dose of the West Coast big office 1950s formula for the future - blancmange architecture with Chevrolet styling. It would be interesting to speculate on the character of Tomorrowland if Walt's backyard chats on architecture with Welton Becket could have been substituted in favour of a dialogue with Konrad Wachsmann. Certainly the 'day after tomorrowland' could have been anticipated and real innovative technology in architecture could have started to match the areas of real technological fascination found in the undercrofts and the macrostructure of the park: the pneumatic tubes of AVAC; the automated trash collection system compacted for centralised dispersal; the water management of 43 square miles of water; the central energy plant computerised for distribution control for natural gas, compressed air, fuel oil and domestic water supplies; the solar energy experiments, the conservation programme, the pest control programme and the completely computerised long-distance telephone system.

Although the Audio-Animatronic performers go about their paces unerringly, the most applauded area of Disney design remains that of the cast. Nowhere on stage or backstage can be found what was once the stereotyped amusement park image - the unshaven barker or the slovenly gum-chewing waitress. Starting with Disneyland in 1955, employee excellence has brought two decades of compliments from public and press alike. Included in the *Wall Street Journal* that reported **'You can see more respectful courteous people at Disney World in one afternoon than in New York in a year'** . . . which makes Charles Moore's cryptic, albeit playful, view of Disneyland more understandable - that when we become more enlightened we will understand **'the multiple realities of Disneyland'** and even come to enjoy our cities as gigantic themeparks.

Walt Disney World

MASTER PLAN
AND TRANSPORTATION PLAN

APRIL, 1980

LAKE MABLE

MAGIC KINGDOM

CONTEMPORARY RESORT   BAY LAKE

SEVEN SEAS LAGOON

SOUTH LAKE

RIVER COUNTRY

POLYNESIAN RESORT

FUTURE DEVELOPMENT

GOLF RESORT

FORT WILDERNESS CAMPGROUND

FUTURE DEVELOPMENT

SSR 535

FUTURE DEVELOPMENT

HOTEL PLAZA

FUTURE WORLD

EPCOT CENTER

CLUBHOUSE

LAKE BUENA VISTA

LIVING TREE FARM

SHOPPING VILLAGE

WORLD SHOWCASE

SSR 535

FUTURE DEVELOPMENT

FUTURE DEVELOPMENT

FUTURE DEVELOPMENT

INTERSTATE 4

LEGEND

Walt Disney World Master Plan

WDW Magic Kingdom Entrance

Tokyo Disneyland

Tokyo Disneyland

Main Street Electrical Parade

Pirates of the Caribbean

Street Vendor WDW

Horse-drawn Carriage WDW

Crystal Palace WDW

Cinderella Fountain

Main Street WDW

Main Street Fireworks

The Haunted Mansion

EPCOT Hieroglyphics

Polynesian Shades

Castle Detail WDW

EPCOT Sistine Ceiling

Adventureland Building

Cinderella Castle WDW

WonderWorld ©

Themepark and Related Industries Development
Corby, Northamptonshire

Context

What is it?

Imagine a place that has as its reasons for existence, entertainment and education. A unique resort set in beautifully landscaped surroundings that blends in perfectly with the neighbouring countryside. That takes into account the British climate and so includes a vast weather-protected centre in the tradition of the Great Exhibition Hall of 1851. A centre where the widest variety of attractions can be housed, each based on a particular theme such as the technology of the day or social or environmental matters. Themes that not only look at our prospects for the future but also at our national heritage of history, folklore and fairytale. An ambitious project, but one that's well under way.
Its name is Wonderworld.

Where is it?

Wonderworld is being developed just to the east of Corby, Northamptonshire, with every due consideration for the environment and character of the countryside. An ideal location in many respects, especially when it comes to accessibility. Corby is situated between the M1 and A1 just north of Kettering. It's 80 miles from London and 55 miles from Birmingham, What's more, a direct route to the continent will be formed by the cross-country M1/A1 link road to Felixstowe, which is 110 miles away on the North Sea coast. So, from virtually any direction Wonderworld will be very easy to reach.

Who's it for?

Wonderworld is a family affair first and foremost. And it is aimed at many different families, as the Wonderworld formula is made up of a broad mix of ingredients designed to appeal to people of differing age groups, backgrounds, tastes and interests.
Wonderworld shouldn't be confused with the seaside style of random distractions such as arcades or roller-coasters. These only offer transient thrills to the thrill-seekers. Nor should Wonderworld, despite its dedication to education, be compared to a museum or exhibition that displays items of interest in a mainly passive way.
The big difference with Wonderworld is that it's an activity centre, with the accent very much on participation. The range of people it will attract will vary from senior citizens to school parties to sports groups - in fact all kinds of people, but with an emphasis on the family.

Why is it?

There's a revolution taking place around us. The trend towards shorter working hours and increased leisure time is more than just possibility: it's happening. The traditional forms of recreation are still being enjoyed, but they will not be enough to fill the sheer abundance of free time. Clearly something more is needed. Active things to do that will provide entertaining and rewarding pastimes as well as something else - a satisfying involvement both with the family and with society as a whole.
This is possible by participation in specially designed activities that will increase awareness and enjoyment and develop a sense of community. Wonderworld aims to provide this kind of involvement.

When is it?

Wonderworld is scheduled to open in its first phase during the summer of 1985 and the starting date on site will be in early 1983. Obviously planning and design activities will gain momentum, with the public being kept in touch with progress all the way along the line.

How will it grow?

Right from conception through to execution, only leading specialists in their fields have been selected. This is a guarantee of the highest standards, and will set the pattern for the future; it is a policy that has attracted other people and companies who wish to become a part of the project. Wonderworld is a continuing story and the opportunities are just as exciting as the uniqueness of the concept that's turned from a fantastic dream into practical reality.

WonderWorld ©

An Introduction to WonderWorld

The Social Case

In the private sector, as in the public sector, workforces and workloads are being reduced and the need to fill the vacuum of spare time will be enormous.

Adequate compensation cannot be provided by today's leisure industries simply supplying *more* **of the self-same leisure time, products, events or facilities.**

Until now, leisure time has been filled with distractions, interludes, entertainments and holidays featuring as respites and rewards for work; and it has been work which has afforded and heightened the pleasure. Traditionally, freetime has been limited, an occasion for doing nothing or next to nothing, for getting away from work, responsibility, thought, effort, the bulk of society, and sometimes even the family. From now on the sheer abundance of leisure time will allow for the complete satisfaction of the individual's interest in traditional, mainly passive pastimes and yet ... leave a void.

It is work substitutes that will be needed to offer everyone a fuller involvement in society and with the family; an involvement that will also increase awareness, commitment and enjoyment and develop a sense of community, through the very act of participation.

The Matching Commercial Case

The massive increase of leisure time is already emerging as the single most important development of our time; it will be the ultimate 'product' of so much progress. And it will affect us all.
Habit is a feature of a static or placid environment.
But who can say that these are either static or placid times, for both recent crises and unexpected surges of progress have played havoc with normal buying habits, trends and lifestyles. Consequently new opportunities for development and growth have been created by major dislocations and sudden advances in society's evolution. Many businesses have attempted to take advantage of the rapid movement towards leisure through sponsorship and the like - forays encouraged by entrenched marketeers attempting to retain their share or, at best, to achieve the odd percent gain which will be heralded as some kind of success in otherwise stalemated wars. These are mere tactical skirmishes which, in most cases, fail to recognise that leisure is destined to become the main time of our lives and the real opportunity for company growth rests in leisure time itself. As we recover from the economic hardships of the recent past we can take comfort and reassurance from the fact that even in a state of depression, new businesses based on leisure and discretionary spending have been able to establish themselves successfully in this country, when founded on worthy and well-conceived products.

The world's major manufacturing corporations have recognised for some time the sense and the importance of proving that 'the giant is friendly'. Overall there has developed a strong feeling that major corporations are nothing but self-seeking monsters imposing their will upon the community. All new technology introduced by them is feared and seen by the public as a new way of taking on still more muscle so as to tighten control, further restrict choice, extract greater dues or shrug off employees. The growing resistance mustered by consumer and environmental action groups has made corporations aware of the need to inform and educate the public ... and *involve* them in the developments of the day. Goodwill is now good for business. The current crop of advertising and corporate campaigns, grants and sponsorships can already be seen as primitive devices - unreliable and inadequate vehicles for company images, jostling for places in the consumer dream.

An Acknowledgement

In the USA themeparks have to a degree answered the public's call for better leisure facilities by offering in pleasant settings a confection of entertainments, interests and mild educational stimulants.
The best example of a themepark is Disney World in Florida. A themepark has a particular dedication and, despite the recent addition of Epcot as an international showcase, Disney World is dedicated in the main to the United States of America, and concentrated within Disney World is everything interesting and exciting associated with that nation.
For this reason the American Tourist Board uses Disney World and its companion Disneyland as features in its campaigns. No attraction, be it natural or man-made -Grand Canyon or New York (to some one is just a hole; to others the other's another) - expresses America better, or even begins to match the global appeal of these parks.
The Disney parks allow you to journey through America's fantasy - fairytales and folklore, the world of Mickey Mouse and friends on the one hand, Davy Crockett and Sitting Bull on the other. They also offer the forum for America to bring alive its history and display its heritage, its arts and its crafts, through features like 'Frontiersland' and the 'Hall of Presidents'. The future is featured too - 21st-century living, displaying scientific and technical innovations, in previews and by visual predictions.
Because of the strong appeal of the Disney parks, acting like a magnet on the emotions of worldwide audiences, major industrial and commercial corporations in the United States have sought inclusion and association with this universally acceptable package
A themepark is an encapsulation of everything notable regarding a nation, therefore the potential for selling the essence extends far beyond the boundaries of the park itself.

Witness the international spread of Disney satellite companies. Each is profitable within its respective market and each one cross-promotes the others, thereby forming a revenue-producing free publicity network which beams into the hearts, homes and high streets of a buying and loving public everywhere. And the magic works. Because the child who wears a Mickey Mouse T-shirt living in a suburb of Tokyo, say, remains a candidate visitor for the Disney themeparks for the rest of his or her life.

In a number of ways the old Disney development philosophy still holds good today; the idea of imagery giving vital energy to the enterprise with the homeland being the prime source; the launching of satellite companies to orbit the themepark like planets around a sun, spreading influence in the process; the basic standards of presentation, quality, cleanliness and value beneath which a new park should not fall - each is typical of time-tested Disney doctrine. And yet there must be recognition that lifestyle changes since the conception of Disney's parks have placed additional demands on those developments planned for the future.

Good as Disney and the best of the other American parks are, they remain fashioned to a model established at a time when work-free periods were exclusively for viewing - not doing - leisure, relaxation and passive pastimes.

A participatory themepark can be the first of a new, maybe the ultimate kind of park.

The overall ambition is to develop a new leisure industry based in and around a themepark dedicated to Great Britain. A wonderworld of features sponsored in part by international corporations, acknowledging the best of Britain's past and present, but particularly the plans and prospects for the future. An exciting presentation in one fine setting, providing pleasure for home and international visitors alike, disseminating information and stimulating thought in the slipstream of enjoyment - as a result of the public's active participation on a grand scale.

For everyone, everything wonderful in a world of its own!

WonderWorld Defined

A themepark is not an amusement park with its random collections of distractions in arcades, seaside-style, with roller-coasters offering cheap thrills to the thrill-seeking segment of the community, comprising mainly adolescents, who cause such an unfavourable impact upon those localities which embrace such developments.

With an amusement park there can be no profitable year-round business for the proprietors or the resident community, as the visitors to such places arrive only during the summer season and at public holiday times and weekends. A themepark at its best is a **themespark**, providing a well-considered range of attractions and facilities for the whole community...at all times of year.

Those themeparks in America which restrict themselves to just one theme, suffer - as do many of the leisure places currently operating in the UK - by not providing a broad base of appeal. This makes it difficult to attract the family group, as each member invariably has individual preferences when it comes to leisure pursuits and interests. Often today family differences are even more marked because of the many influences brought to bear on the individual. The sheer pace of progress has the additional effect of time-freezing the generations in different ages with essentially different attitudes. Greater awareness and financial independence have further contributed to the situation where, in the main, the only thing a family now has in common is a name.

A multi-themed leisure place which provides the right blend of facilities and offers a variety of attractions and interests will as a result reward its proprietors and sponsors. The family will be able to democratically agree to visits without compromise or trade-off, or without suffering loss of dissatisfied members. Also, the best mix will allow for other groups within the community to visit at their own preferred times, spreading and creating layers of attendance over more hours of more days. School parties, sports groups, businessmen forming conventions, the Darby and Joan club, housewives, clubs, societies, tourists, holidaymakers, adult education and casual groups are all worthy candidates for a place. The facility which can incorporate features aimed to appeal right across the spectrum - allowing for the public's active participation - has its future secured.

Obviously the passive, loose-linked relationships between sponsoring corporations and themeparks in the States offer a measure of shared benefit and some comfort. But these bonuses pale into insignificance against the marvellous prospect of major corporations and institutions meeting at a park with the public in a pertinent and participatory way.

The benefits to corporations and institutions featured in Wonderworld would come as a result of an active participating public who would discover exciting things to do in precisely themed presentations. These would provide the incentive for the public to acquire a better understanding of the corporations behind the presentations, their roles, responsibilities, progress and future plans destined to affect us all.

Collectively, a spread of companies will be able to provide a wide range of themes born out of their businesses for the public to be part of and so enjoy. And companies will benefit in a number of ways by their association with this centre of goodwill. Some corporations will operate commercially from within Wonderworld, whilst offering facilities for the public to view, and importantly, to participate in some related, informative way. Others will introduce, with the chance of participation, specific entertainments and an education within aptly themed presentations. This contact with the public will be commercially and socially rewarding and will help the public to achieve a higher level of awareness and appreciation of the corporations concerned.

In America, Disney parks provide a compliment to those things America feels happy about and offer compensation for what it lacks. A Disney park compliments the American lifestyle, energy and thrust and compensates for its shallow reservoir of history and heritage. As there is insufficient real evidence of an American past to satisfy the interest, the historical recreations and fabrications featured in themeparks in the States are most valid.

However, with a British themepark the stress of presentation should be on today and the prospects of tomorrow, for we as a breed remain quite relaxed about our ancestry.

The real and abundant evidence around us of a rich and colourful past effectively portrays to a world's audience the British Isles as an historical themepark built out of reality and blended together beautifully over many centuries. There is no room for imitation.

As a nation, however, we continue to demonstrate our anxiety and misgivings about the new developments of the day, and worse - the threatened developments of tomorrow. It is in this respect that a presentation in Wonderworld can bring enlightenment. Add to Wonderworld those episodes or aspects of our past which have neither a physical existence in reality nor in any way duplicate those other themes on show elsewhere - and refreshingly new presentations will be made.

So the planned British park acknowledges Disney...but is dedicated to Britain with its stress on the future... and with the special plus of participation as the offer.

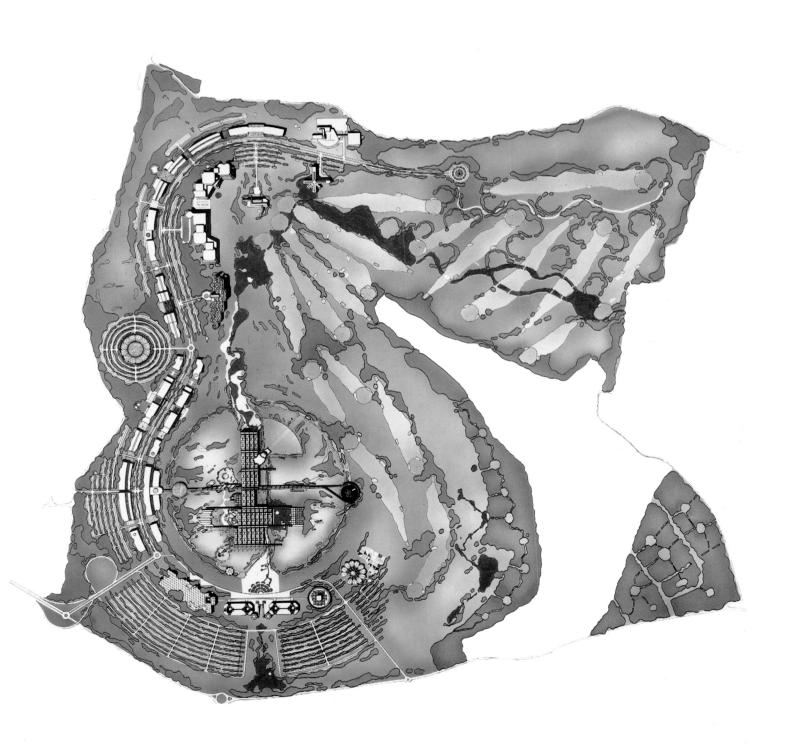

Site Plan

The Theme Building

The site presents a variety of engineering and architectural challenges and opportunities. The site comprises three zones of very different character:

1. an area of land to the east worked for minerals and subsequently restored
2. a broad area of unworked agricultural land to the north and west
3. a valley between the interface of the mineral workings and the restored areas and traversing north-south in the length of the site.

The main factors influencing the development of the site were the varying levels and ground conditions. It proved possible to combine these conditions with the local environmental factors. Thus a linear form of support development to the main themepark follows the southern, western and part of the northern boundaries using wherever possible the good load-bearing ground. The land adjacent to the north eastern and eastern boundaries or 'country' edge of the site which is unsuitable for economic construction is developed as a recreational area containing an international golf course.

The themepark, set in its own bowl, is the hub of the site, straddling the valley and linking the flanks of the development. The building housing the majority of the themes is enclosed, thereby ensuring year round comfort for visitors. The building lies in the centre of the bowl along the line of the exposed bedrock and rides the contours linking the high and the low ground. The contours of the land allow for a continuous concrete undercroft to be constructed, running the length of the building and built directly on the exposed rockface. This undercroft contains servicing access maintenance areas and public escape routes from above. Two major stepped levels above allow free pedestrian movement along the 450 metre length of the building. The structure is divided into six major spans each 64.8 metres long. This allows a columnless space for each theme or group of themes. The secondary span across the building is 16.2m. The roof plane steps down with the slope of the land 2.7m at each 16.2m increment. The large spans are possible by suspending the roof from town clusters in the 8.1 metre structural zone between each theme location. Cross-pedestrian circulation is contained in this zone linking high to low ground. The structure above the undercroft is a modular grid system of tubular steel components ensuring speed of erection and ease of phasing. Simple detailing ensures an economic solution in a visibly exciting and readable form.

The main building volume will be space heated with individually localised air conditioning in attraction areas. Heavy plant and theme pavilion air-handling plant will be located in the undercroft, high level plant areas will be contained in the structural zones. A medium pressure gas ring main will feed modular boilerhouses in the undercroft. All heating and hot water will be by gas firing. Heating distribution will be by medium pressure hot water. Humidification will be by steam. All areas will have an integrated sprinkler system for the protection of the theme buildings and individual themes.

Power distribution will be from 11 kv/415V ring main in the undercroft. Load centres will be controlled from the central desk, with systems monitoring by central computer with constant modulators for maximum efficiency.

High and medium lighting will be by high pressure sodium and mercury vapour, as appropriate, with fluorescent and tungsten for effect lighting in theme areas with low energy lasers for special effects.

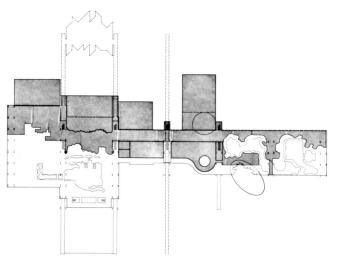

UPPER CONCOURSE LEVEL

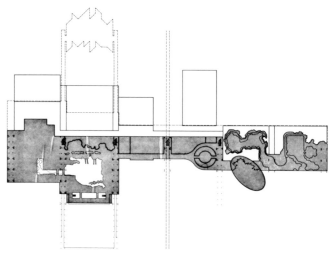

LOWER CONCOURSE LEVEL

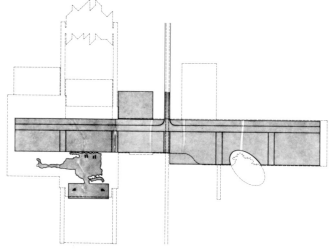

UNDERCROFT LEVEL

Theme Building Floor Plans

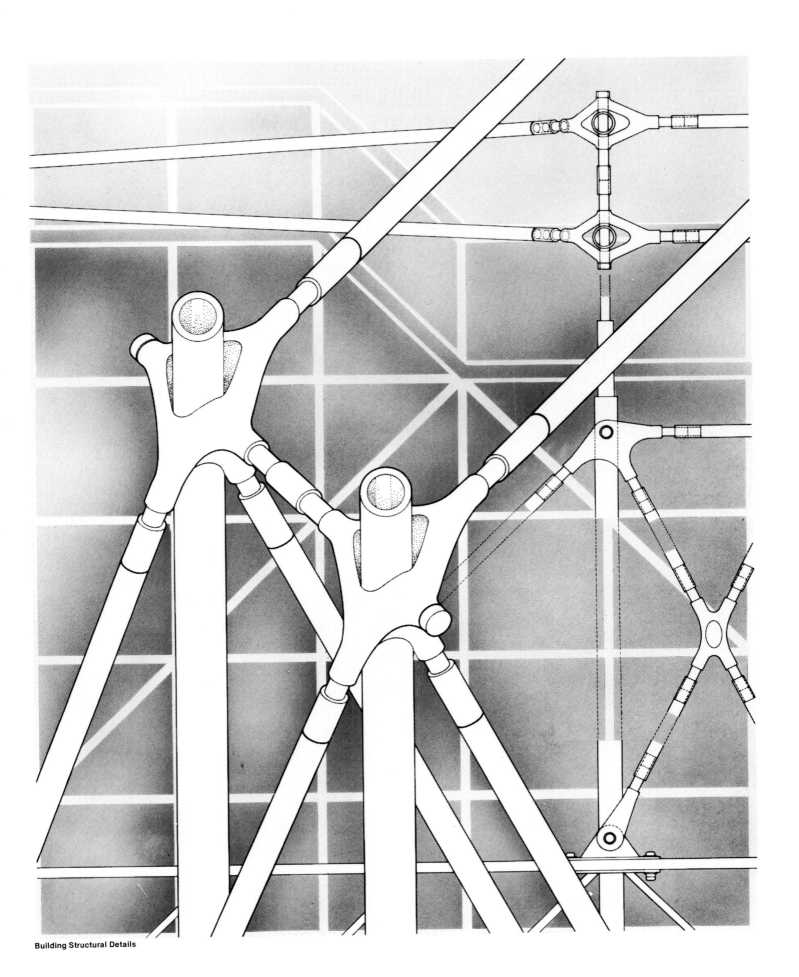

Building Structural Details

Theme Building Plan

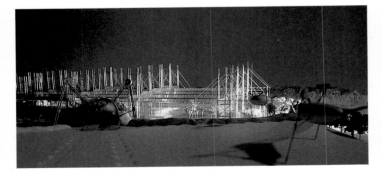

Theme Building. Some Views

Derek Walker
Concept and Reality

The Shape of Things To Come

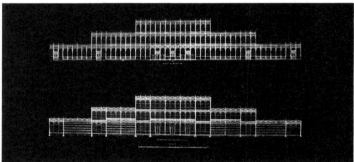
The Crystal Palace 1851

The Palm House, Kew Gardens

Krypton City

John Pastier wrote an article in the AIA Journal in 1978 entitled 'The Architecture of Escapism'. I was fascinated by its contents and one particular paragraph has remained impressed on my memory—it read: 'We may sing the praises of opera and poetry, but when we vote with out feet we are far more likely to find ourselves standing in Disney World or Las Vegas than in the Lincoln or Kennedy Centre.'

Long before Robert Venturi, courtesy of Tom Wolfe, took his Yale students to Las Vagas and interpreted the delights of the Strip, or prior to Peter Blake's uncritical praise of Disney World as America's new found town philosophy, Mr. & Mrs. American Public who recognise a real playground when they see one, had already made their own decisions. In America the maxim is to shoot not just for the best, but for the most effective. In a pragmatic America, Disney Productions is perhaps the greatest monument to pragmatism. Its aim is to provide the greatest pleasure for the greatest number, which means they shoot for the middle nine times out of ten. The quality of aim is not in question, judging by the 14,000,000 attendance at Disney World in 1981, and the resounding success of the Disney Theme Park since Disneyland opened in 1955.

My fascination with the Disney legend is like my continual delighted surprise at the City of Los Angeles, which elevates the art of the impossible to the commonplace, where skills of illusion and fetish finish are available through the movies, the aircraft industry and in turn are stretched by the ultimate consumer society in that city.

When John Hench, Executive Vice President of WED Enterprises explained the Disney organisation's interest in psychology, subliminal impressions and the evolutionary value of harmonious surrounding, a more disturbing series of apprehensions comes to mind. One imagines a Disneyesque sorcerer playing one's unconcious like a pocket computer, punching in childhood triumphs and tribal anxieties. The themed entertainment experience begins to sound less like pricey fun and more like inexpensive therapy. But at what point does skilful entertainment turn to dangerous abuse? How do you abuse harmony? Hench replies 'How do you give people too much sense of well being—in a properly ordered environment' he continues, 'the message is wholly accurate. Look how people who live in cities have to go somewhere in the country for recreation and when that sense of natural order creeps back into their views they are quite different people. They will actually start to talk to each other again. If the only images present at Disneyland were of funny animals, the mechanics of reassurance would not be effective—it is necessary to supply threats and disarm them, to defray the worst demons and make a world demonstrably safe for the funny animals to play in... The essential message of Disneyland is that there is nothing to fear...'

But what has this to do with the concept and reality of Wonderworld? In a design sense very little, but in an atmospheric sense a great deal. People are not so much aware of specific building design or colour as they are of atmosphere or impression that is conveyed to them through an overall park design.

The first lesson from Disney is the need for one team to co-ordinate all aspects of development including site selection, themeing, landscaping, building design and construction, interior design, colour and graphics and even food and merchandise planning.

The second lesson, and in sloppy, feckless Britain, the key to potential success, is the comprehensive role of management to ensure that nothing is done to disrupt the image and atmosphere created. Intrusions such as litter and vandalism are obvious dangers. Great emphasis must be placed on the training of both permanent and temporary staff who are important contributions to the atmosphere. For example, the Disney personnel code admonishes 'You are not an employee, but a performer on stage at all times. Walt Disney presents you. Leave your worries and cares outside. Put on a smile.'

If we acknowledge the debt any theme park designer or developer owes to Disney Organisation as the pioneer who gave themepark success and legitimacy, the perfectionist who sets the pace in quality, product and management skills, the introduction of one word, 'climate', explains why our physical solution for Wonderworld responds to a different drummer and looks back for inspiration to a different age.

At 6 o'clock on 30th November 1936 England lost, arguably, the most remarkable and innovative building of the 19th century, the 'Crystal Palace' which had been a magnet for the world in 1851 and for Londoners in subsequent years until 1936. Paxton's building was not only beautiful, it was remarkably flexible—about one million square feet of space. In 1851 it housed nearly 14,000 exhibitors and over 100,000 exhibits. It had the dimensions to cope with fully grown elm trees in the South West transept and was visited by 6,000,000 people in that year. Its move to Sydenham was no less astonishing. A great seawater aquarium was built in 1872. It also contained schools of Art, Science, Literature, Music and Engineering.

It was at Crystal Palace that for the first time ever, a large audience watched moving pictures, for in 1868 a huge Aoetrope, turned by a gas engine, was installed. There was a parrot house, an aviary, a monkey house, a club, an orangery and a large Victoria Cross gallery. Balloon ascents were a regular favourite attraction, and of course, Mr. Blondin made a visit and cooked an omelette on the high wire.

It was an ideal place for shows and exhibitions—they followed each other with ever increasing frequency. Rose shows, pigeon and poultry shows, cat and dog shows, trade fairs, electrical exhibitions, art exhibitions, aeronautical, mining and photographic exhibitions. The special exhibitions were held in the main body of the building, in the galleries and in the grounds.

It became a place for mass meetings of societies of every shade and description. There were music festivals, mass bands, circuses and pantomime. In other words, the Crystal Palace had all the dimensional criteria and flexibility to fulfil a role as the envelope for the first theme park …

In essence, then, the external inspirations of the Wonderworld venture has developed from the mainipulative marketing and management base of Disney which has produced a new formula including an enclosure with flexibility and linked additives inspired by 'Paxton's Palace'.

'Wonderworld' is the product of several years of research into the British, European and American leisure industry by Group Five and the concept development for a major Theme Park was done in parallel during this period.

In 1981 the nucleus of the development team was commissioned for the development and a number of prospective sites had already been identified. No place in Britain can readily accommodate a Themepark on the scale they had envisaged — there is insufficient slack built into the system of travel ways, services and hospitality facilities to justify the selection of any particular location. To a degree, such an acknowledgement has a liberating effect in the absence of a ready made location. Anywhere in the main body of Britain will do. The reason for not wishing to be placed out on a limb was to maximise the opportunity for as many UK residents as possible to have access to the Park in terms of travel time. A location accessible for Continental visitors was also considered to be desirable.

The reason for the choice of Corby specifically was the positive attitude displayed by the Local and County Authorities and the Commission for the New Towns to the idea of the park being developed there. It can therefore be said that within the widest marketing constraints, the selection was essentially emotional.

A pre-feasibility study on 'Wonderworld' was undertaken by Coopers and Lybrand in September 1980. This study embraced all aspects of the proposed development and indicated that Corby, situated in the heart of Central England and 80 miles from London, 50 miles from Birmingham, 45 miles from Cambridge and 112 miles from Felixstowe, would be a suitable location. The proposed M1-A1 link road would further enhance its accessibility.

Group Five have always believed that the expertise required to design 'Wonderworld' existed within the United Kingdom. The essential contribution which a 'Design Team' could make to 'Wonderworld' was to translate Group Five's concept, themes, philosophy and marketing strategy into a master plan. Following considerable research by Group Five on the consultancy services available in the United

Kingdom, Derek Walker Associates were appointed as Architect/Planners for 'Wonderworld'.

Each theme was developed in terms of content, concept and marketing strategy, with dimensional criteria established for attractions, commercial outlets, restaurants and support systems.

At the macro scale a theme park is virtually a New Town dedicated to leisure. It has to be environmentally attractive, clean, comfortable, and friendly.

The physical attributes of the site provided the catalyst for the conceptual approach.

The site of some 1,000 acres located to the East of Corby, near Weldon Village, enjoys fine views over the surrounding countryside. The land has been quarried for iron ore and limestone and the Eastern half of the site has been reinstated over a period of years.

Central to the site is a rift valley which is formed at the interface between the recently mined areas and the reinstated areas. Surveys indicate that the valley would bisect a Theme Park mandala of 700m diameter, which was the optimum scale required for the containment of the themed areas for 'Wonderworld'. The contours of the land offered an ideal opportunity to design an enclosure utilising the valley base for a two level service and storage zone. This undercroft zone also provided the anonymous volume of space needed for the ride attractions.

The faceted levels running laterally across the site created with economy the multi level sculptured base of the main building. Added modelling was introduced in the roofscape as individual themed areas required considerable height variation ranging from intimacy to grandeur. This formal need gave the opportunity to cascade the suspended roof form across the slope of the site, linking the closed and opened linear facades. The rift valley edge tended to contain the ride caverns and zones of artificial lighting and the configurations of roof design allowed for varying levels of transparency to confirm with the specific functional needs below.

Prior to the commencement of the detail design on individual themes, a general arrangement strategy was agreed with Group Five. This responded to alternative concepts phased and linked to the specific themed elements and external support systems on the West boundary of the site. The support systems included administrative offices, warehousing, TV buildings, commercial and hospitality zones. With the agreement on general arrangement, two areas of development were released for both consultant and client.

The macro scale elements include structural concepts for the main building with Ove Arup & Partners, lightweight structures for the additive elements with Buro Happold, the transportation and off-site Civil Engineering with Brian Colquhoun & Partners. These three engineering practices, together with Quantity Surveyors Widnell & Trollope, constituted the initial appointments in a long ranging consultancy strategy which will see a number of other architectural and engineering consultants such as Foster Associates and Frei Otto commissioned for individual buildings in the support and hospitality area.

The development of the themes provides one of the greatest pleasures on this complex and massive project—the opportunity to work with a much more diverse and inventive group of contributors than most architectural projects provide.

In essence themeing is not just invention, but it appropriately puts to work talents whose links with architecture have usually been peripheral. We have a country with a plethora of obsessive and eccentric talents, and Group Five have woven them into the fabric of 'Wonderworld's' themed concepts.

The quality of 'teamwork' we can achieve will obviously reflect the eventual quality of the park. The project has enough content to offer opportunities at every level with the consequent blurring of professional skills dimumition of architectural ego—innovative, structural and mechanical engineering, well researched building science and components, energy systems, transportation and movement development, communications, theatre, special effects, graphics, lighting, security, landscaping—it becomes in a sense another Festival of Britain—a singular celebration of quality, of design skill and invention. It can combine skills without compromise and offers a look at the future which is both participatory and educational!

At the time of going to press the following Companies have joined the Design Team: French Kier Construction Limited and Drake and Scull Engineering Limited.

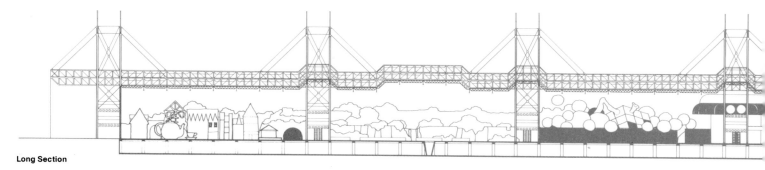

Long Section

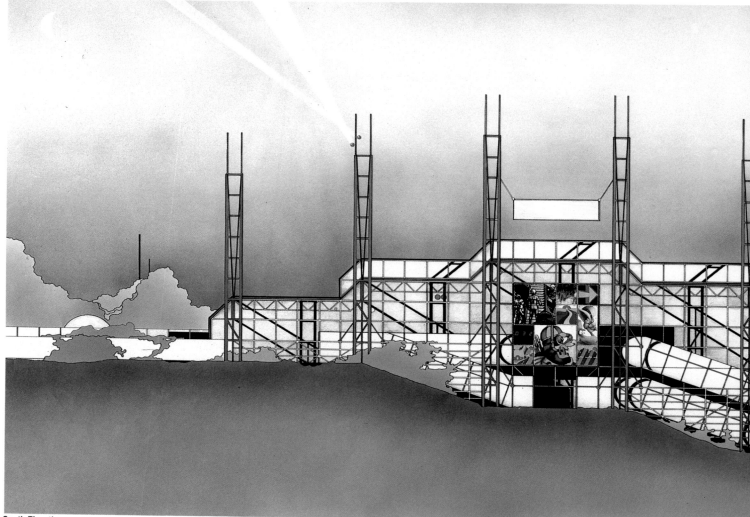

South Elevation

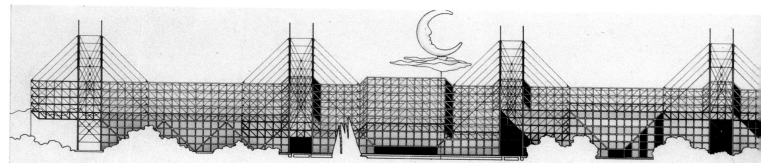

East Elevation

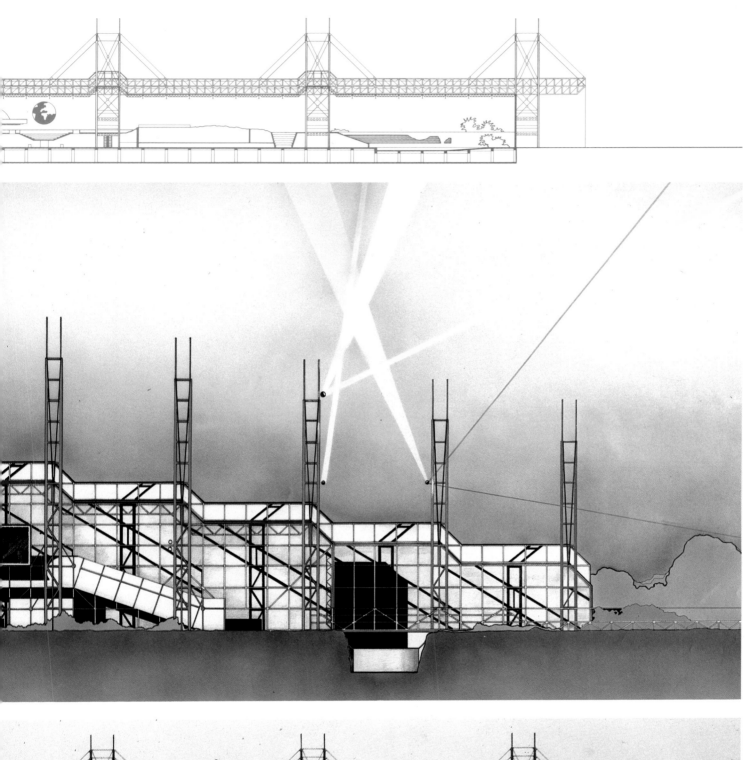

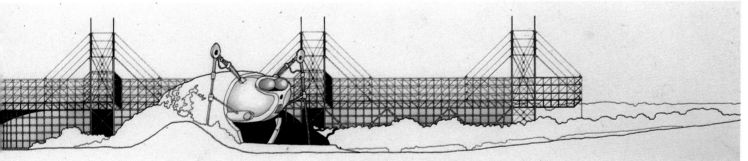

13

LAND: hope and glory

For thousands of years the land of Britain has been cultivated and nurtured to yield an abundance of the crops, fruits, vegetables and healthy livestock that are famous the world over. The agricultural quality of the land is complemented by a wealth of natural flora and fauna - a heritage that's jealously guarded by those concerned with the preservation of the environment.

This land, as a nation, can also claim a rich culture that has grown from indigenous talents as well as those that have settled from other lands and flowered in its healthy climate. As a result, great ideas and thoughts have been expressed in a wonderfully eloquent language, spoken throughout the world.

The essential character of a highly individual land is to be found in Wonderworld's Land Pavilion. There will be a wide variety of special presentations ranging from the perennial favourite 'Wind in the Willows' and Tolkien's 'The Lord of the Rings' to David Bellamy's 'Countryside Safari'. Of special interest will be a junior computer park in conducive surroundings. Here will be offered a unique chance for many to try their hands and stretch their minds with modern computers. A full range of subjects and interests will be embraced, especially programs showing how technology under proper control can benefit ecology.

LAND   THEME LOCATION

INGREDIENTS: LAND
- ● David Bellamy's Countryside Safari
- Great Greenhouse
- Computer Park
- Ratty's River Ride
- Sherlock Holmes' Mystery
- Battle Ground Cinema
- 'The Lord of the Rings' Adventure
- ▲ Sherwood Forest Restaurant
- Snack Bar
- Farmhouse Food
- ■ Land Emporium:
- Poster and Bric-à-brac Market
- British Heritage Bookshop
- Garden and Flower Shop
- Soda Fountain
- Casual Clothing Store
- ◆ Rock and Mineral Mine
- ◆ Service Facilities

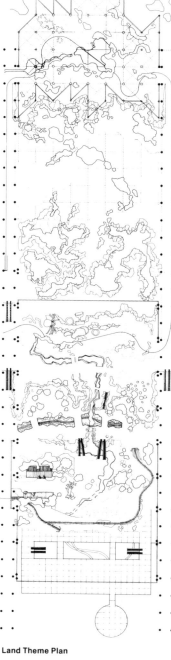

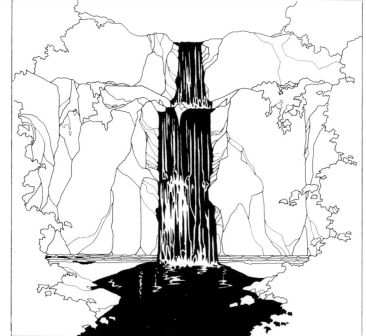

The Waterfall

Computer Park. A natural introduction to modern technology.

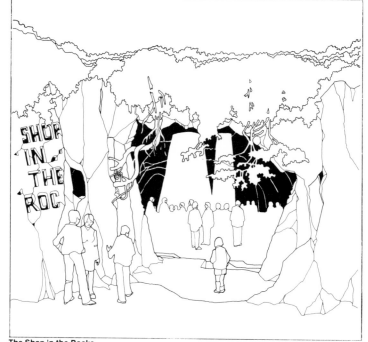

The Shop in the Rocks

Land Theme Plan

Land Theme Approach

The canary-coloured cart, their pride and joy,
lay on its side in the ditch,
an irredeemable wreck

A place where heroes could fitly feast after victory

Toad is rather rich, you know, and this is really
one of the nicest houses in these parts

"Poop-poop"

They gathered round the glowing embers
of the great wood fire

set them to capture the old grey horse

"There's Toad Hall"

"I've done with carts for ever"

"Believe me, my young friend,
there is nothing - absolutely nothing -
half so much worth doing as simply
messing about in boats. Simply messing"

Toad has ordered a large
and very expensive motor-car

Rounding a bend in the river

While the moon, serene and detached in a cloudless sky,
did what she could

What seemed at first sight like
a little landlocked lake

They could see Otter start up,
tense and rigid

So beautiful and strange and new!
O, Mole! the beauty of it!
The merry bubble and joy

with uplifted voice he sang,
to the enraptured audience

The field-mice and harvest-mice seemed preoccupied

"It's my world, and I don't want any other.
What it hasn't got is not worth having,
and what it doesn't know is not worth knowing".

He did his best, but he was a fat animal

sat down by his side
in the cool herbage

A fat, wicker
luncheon-basket

The afternoon sun was getting low
as the Rat sculled gently
homewards in a dreamy mood

The rush of air in his face,
the hum of the engine

"It's quite a long time since
you did any poetry"

little boat painted blue outside and white within

A full-fed river. Never in his life had he seen a river before -
this sleek, sinuous, full-bodied animal,
chasing and chuckling, gripping things with a gurgle
and leaving them with a laugh

The barge-woman was gesticulating wildly
and shouting, "Stop, stop, stop!"

Jumping off all his four legs at once,
in the joy of living

PASSENGER LOADING/UNLOADING

A pleasant trip in a blue and white boat through 'The Wind in the Willows' countryside on a summer's day.

Endless reflections in the glade of the Sherwood Forest restaurant. The place for a really good tuck in!

David Bellamy wants to get you into flowers during a Tom Thumb size safari of the British countryside.

'An adventure based on Paul Raymond Gregory's paintings inspired by "The Lord of the Rings".'

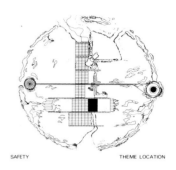
SAFETY   THEME LOCATION

SAFETY: for home and road

Add the high incidence of accidents in the home to our familiarly depressing road casualty figures and it becomes apparent that there's a need for a more effective safety programme. It's very much in the public interest as well as concerning those in government departments and commercial institutions whose policy it is to support a wide variety of safety projects.

Popular themes, imagery and characterisation have all been used - but at Wonderworld a fresh approach will be taken. A whole area dedicated to safety gives visitors in any age group the opportunity to test themselves in ways that are challenging, informative - and fun. After all, it's a problem that affects us all.

INGREDIENTS: SAFETY
● Safety Park and Danger Zone
　History of Transport Cinema
▲ Highland Pullman Restaurant Car
　Drive-in Restaurant
　Safety Cat Milk Bar
■ Car Emporium
　Shunter's Shop
　Safety Cat's Shop
◆ Service Facilities

The Great Greenhouse, a place of beauty and tranquility.

Holmes safety. Unravelling the mysteries of home safety and insurance, Sherlock style. To your amazement and that of Dr Watson.

The Great Greenhouse

Safety Cat car simulators. With a variety of programs test how street-wise you are . . . important for cats with only one life!

RHYME: the lost village

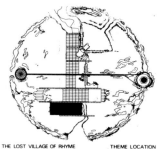

Everyone is promised a Rhyme royal reception in Wonderworld.

THE LOST VILLAGE OF RHYME   THEME LOCATION

For hundreds of years British nursery rhymes have appealed to and delighted successive generations. The ones we know today - and the wonderful characters introduced to us through rhymes - have proven themselves to be the best, most memorable and robust, living on from a long-gone time, indicating for them the real prospect of immortality.

And it is the nursery which has protected rhymes and kept them full of life. Try to vary a rhyme and outraged children will get you to tell it again - properly. Whilst the rhymes must stay the same, the characters will positively benefit from fresh interpretations thereby increasing appeals to the newest generations.

Waiting to be discovered in Wonderworld will be the Lost Village of Rhyme, a fantasy homeplace for the multitude of colourful characters which we have all grown to love through softly spoken words, song or our first solo flights with the printed page.

Mixed into this fascinating setting will be other aspects of traditional village life. The arts and crafts that for centuries have been part of the British scene will be found to be alive and well in their Wonderworld home. An opportunity for everyone to observe and maybe try their hand or, with an extended stay, learn a craft from the masters.

INGREDIENTS: LOST VILLAGE
● Reverend Awdry's Red Engine Ride
Alan Aldridge's 'Butterfly Ball'
The Rhyme Time Theatre
The Shoe House Ride
Father Christmas Land Ride
Gulliver Giant Playground
Minature Village
Crooked House of Illusion
Crooked Street
Windmill
Watermill
The Lost Village Square
including:
Dickory Dock's Clock Tower
Mother Goose's House
Bandstand
▲ Tea Pot Store and Tea Room
Station Break
Tommy Tucker's Ice Cream Parlour
Jack Sprat's Restaurant
'Rhyme Time' Restaurant
Corner Shop Confectionery Stand
Pumpkin Restaurant
■ News Stand
Souvenir Emporium:
Gift Shop
Book Shop
Record and Tapes
Village Post Office
Country Market Hall
Quite Contrary Silk Flower Shop
Card and Stationery Shop
House of Magic
Cup and Saucer Fine China
Holiday Accessories Shop
Children's Accessories Shop
Tobacconist
Baby Care Shop
Stroller Shop
◆ Wonderworld Information
High Street Bank
Baby Care Centre
Camera Centre
Stroller and Wheelchair Rental
First Aid Centre
Service Facilities

INGREDIENTS: CRAFT SQUARE
● The Blacksmith's Forge
The Buttery
The Shadow Box
Photo Fantasy Booth
The Workshops:
Woodturner
Thatcher
Potter
Quilter
Weaver
Glass-blower
Musical Instrument Maker
Jeweller
Leather Craft
▲ The Kitchens:
Candy Confectionery
Jam and Preserves
Bottled Country Fruits
Bakery
Pastry Shop and Kitchen
Beverage Stand
Georgie Porgie's Chestnut and Roast
Potato Kiosk
■ Clock Shop
Garden Ornament Shop
Barber's Shop
◆ Service Facilities

Rhyme Village Plan

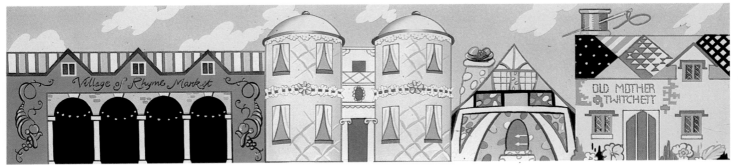

Rhyme Village. Where wonderful characters influence the character of the buildings.

Perspective View of Rhyme Village Square

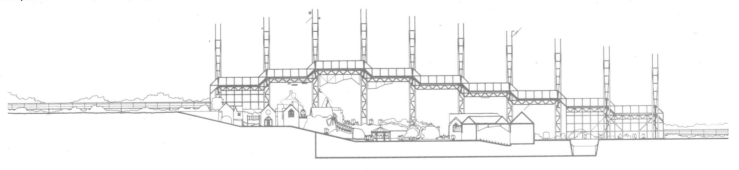

Rhyme Section

Little Jack Horner   The Giant

Little Boy Blue   Jack Sprat and his Wife   The Humptys

          The Little Dog   Jack and Jill   The Knave   The King of Hearts

                                                                                                    Polly

Rhyme villagers.

Hey diddle diddle, The cat and the fiddle, The cow jumped over the moon; The little dog

The Cat (and the Fiddle)

The Cow   The Moon

Mother Goose

Tom, Tom the Piper's Son   Georgie Porgie

Wayne Sheep

Bo Peep's Sheep
Meryl Sheep, Gary the Lamb, Barbara Lamb, Sean Sheep

Curly Locks and her Lockettes

Wee Willie Winkie

The Crooked Man

Old Mother Hubbard

The Dish and the Spoon

laughed to see such sport, And the dish ran away with the spoon.

A giant attraction. Gulliver makes Rhyme village look Lilliput in Wonderworld.

Made small, and whisked away, up through the chimney to the North Pole...

You'll be more than a little chuffed to be in the company of Thomas, Edward or Henry as they huff and puff you round the Park.

...where you'll visit Father Christmas and helpers in his workshop stocking up.

Craft Square Axonometric

You're cordially invited to the Butterfly Ball. A wonderful chance to meet Alan Aldridge's beautiful bugs and their fabulous friends in a fairytale setting.

AIR AND SPACE: flights of fancy

Remarkable achievements in the air and in space form a significant part of Britain's history. Unfortunately, the past, however recent, has little appeal to youngsters - of any era. They're attracted by the heroes and developments of the day and still more attracted by the promise of the super happenings of tomorrow. It would be a sad day if they failed to appreciate the ways in which yesterday has helped shape the future.

Wonderworld will renew their interest by showing the important events in aerospace - past, present and future. It will use the latest technology and methods of presentation to enable people to re-enact and actually be part of the experience. A new, enjoyable and very stimulating learning process.

How today's technology brings the past to life.

The Battle of Britain was the turning point of the Second World War. At Wonderworld the drama and the need for split-second action are re-created in a situation where you are the fighter pilot. See what he would have seen from his cockpit. Hear what he would have heard through his headphones, as well as the sounds of battle outside. What better way to remember the facts of history than by experiencing them yourself.

The way to the stars ... and beyond

Science fiction has introduced space flight and technology to enthusiastic generations who have received an education in the process. Wonderworld's presentation will include flight simulators and incredible special effects that add a new dimension - a time machine that can transport you to the future or the past.

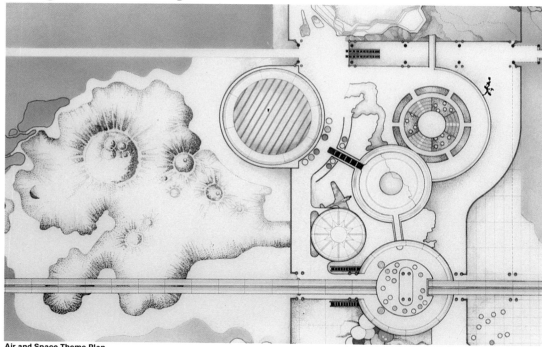

Air and Space Theme Plan

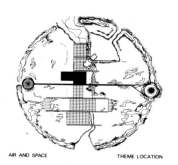

AIR AND SPACE   THEME LOCATION

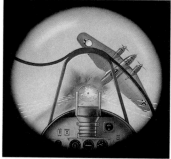

Combat simulator!

INGREDIENTS: AIR AND SPACE
● Arthur C. Clarke's 'Mysterious Universe'
  Patrick Moore's Astronomy Dome
  Battle of Britain Simulation
  Cinema of Flight
  Space City Operational Area
  Space Trip
  Planetarium
  Space Workshop
▲ Ace Canteen
■ Space City Far Out Foods
  Great Air and Space Emporia:
  Kits, Kites, Books
  Models, Memorabilia
  Cards, Clothes, Games
  Spitfire Photo Fantasy Booth
◆ Service Facilities

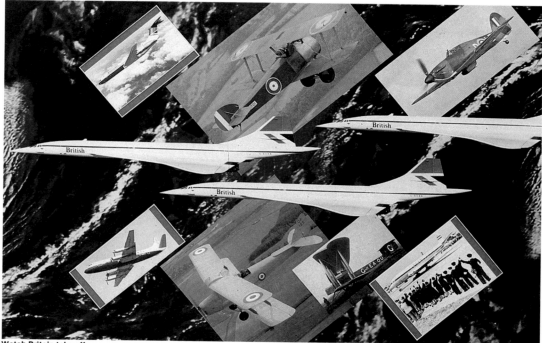

Watch Britain take off.

24

Out of this world via the Patrick Moore observatory.

Patrick Moore's own sketches of Mars and Saturn obtained from his 12½ reflector telescope.

The planetarium, a space workshop, a working model of the galaxy and even space 'tours' will be under the directorship of Patrick Moore.

25

Arthur C. Clark invites you to ...

...journey through the mysterious universe in style ...

COMMUNICATIONS: sailing messages across the airwaves

Communications are undoubtedly among the major influences on our way of life. Not just the systems that make sure we get the message, but the media that carry the message · whether it's information, education, entertainment, images or dreams.

We are in an age where communications can create, as well as satisfy, our needs and desires. This applies as much to big business as it does to small everyday pleasures. This is only made possible by technological advances, yet it is a fear of technology itself that often clouds the public's full appreciation of the benefits and the scope of communications.

There is clearly a need to explain to people just how the systems aid business as well as provide information and entertainment. And how in the future they will lead to even further improvements in out lifestyle.

When planning the Communications Centre, much thought was given to ensuring that it does not become dated. Even Disney's 'Tomorrowland' today looks distinctly yesteryear. So the space city architecture of Frank Hampson, creator of Dan Dare, was chosen. Conceived in the late 1940s, his work still has the same futuristic appeal · protected from the ageing process by its special wrap of fantasy.

Dan Dare ... Frank Hampson's creation, one of the all-time greats of comic-book art.

DIY TV where professionals help you get your school or society production taped.

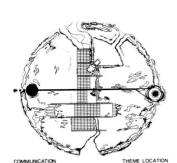

COMMUNICATION   THEME LOCATION

INGREDIENTS: COMMUNICATIONS
- ● Commercial Radio Station
- DIY Recording Studio
- Razzamatazz Territory
- Film Showcase
- Special Effects Studio
- Print Works
- DIY TV Studio
- Professional TV Studio
- Monorail
- ▲ Dan Dare Restaurant
- Radio Fun Food
- ■ Dan Dare Emporium:
- Books, Cards
- Souvenirs, Space Kits
- Action Toys
- Wonderworld Post Office
- ◆ Service Facilities

See a professional TV studio at work where production takes shape by a process of cutting, dubbing, mixing, tuning, pruning, polishing and presenting.

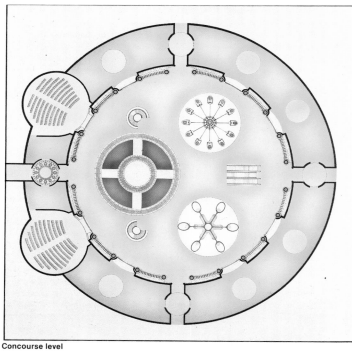

Concourse level

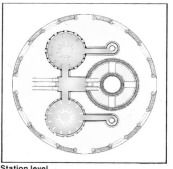

Station level

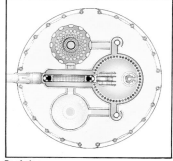

Roof plan

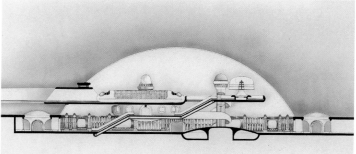

Communications Station Section

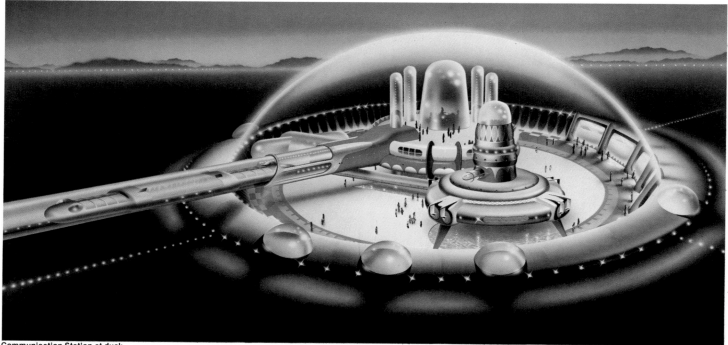

Communication Station at dusk.

Razzamataz Territory. A children's adventure land.

Let the professionals put you on record just for fun . . . or for real.

The commercial radio station where you could get the chance to DJ.

The Dan Dare restaurant is where the Treen tureen serves anything from a Mekonburger to an Anastasia cocktail.

THE BODY: the inside story

The 'How it works' format has always had a magnetic pull with its easy-to-understand and inviting style of presentation. Even if the observer is just casually interested in the subject he'll be drawn, but when this format is applied to something as fascinating as the human body, it's irresistible. However, this will be no ordinary demonstration or explanation - it's a fantastic voyage where the travellers ride in weird and wonderful craft through the anatomy.

But it's a giant body with a difference - hardly surprising when you learn that it's been designed by Terry Gilliam in true Monty Python style. Once this rather unusual guided tour is over, travellers will be treated to a spectacular and dramatic programme by Dr Jonathan Miller. With the most advanced visual effects, using as its standard reference 'The Body in Question', the mysteries of the human make-up are told in the most informative and entertaining way yet.

Covered too, will be the power of the senses, in Professor Gregory's Sensorama: the significance of diet; the positive benefits of drugs and medicine, as well as many more items that everyone will want to know about. Examples include the importance of maintenance, condition, exercise and repair. As the subject is one that's close to all our hearts, the journey will have great appeal for young and old alike.

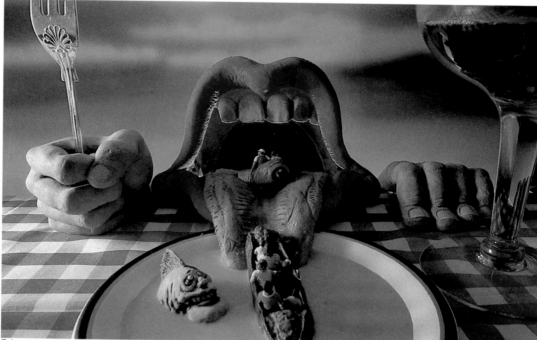

Take a crazy cruise through the body in a carrot canoe, banana boat or sausage ship...

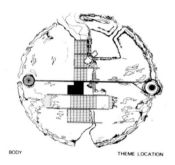

BODY   THEME LOCATION

INGREDIENTS: BODY
- ● The Body Trip
- Jonathan Miller's 'The Body in Question'
- Professor Gregory's Sensorama
- Video Games
- ▲ Health Food Restaurant
- Terry Gilliam's Restaurant
- Drug Store
- ■ Health Food Shop
- Body Trip Memorabilia
- Apothecary
- Photo Fantasy Booth
- Major First Aid Centre
- ◆ Service Facilities

A ride where your heart enters your mouth.

A Turtle burger...
or a Steak sandwich

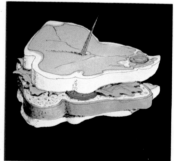

Terry Gilliam's restaurant where junk food takes on a new meaning!

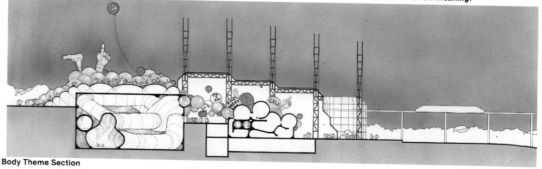

Body Theme Section

30

The Body in Question. Jonathan Miller provides the answers and makes learning fun.

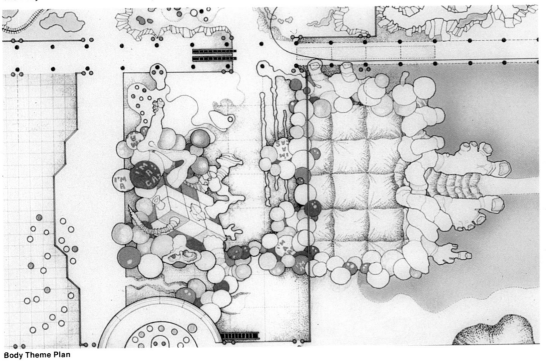

Body Theme Plan

Professor Gregory's Sensorama will stimulate the senses in sensational style.

CONCERT HALL: theme tuned

Theme music...

Hearing, seeing, breathing music...

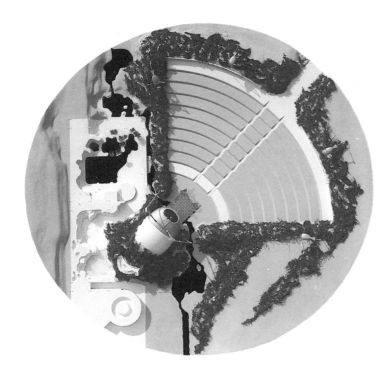

Throughout the years, music has helped the world go round, but today those concerned in the listening as well as the performing have become much more discriminating. This has put new demands on traditional venues in terms of acoustics, facilities and presentation. Since each style of music has its own culture and stars, a massive international industry has grown up in the process.

Within the themepark development there's a great advantage in having a complex suitable for all kinds of music. So there will be the Jeff Wayne Concert Hall - dramatically styled to reflect visually his 'The War of the Worlds' hit album. Unlike many concert halls, this will be fully employed. Themed productions for Wonderworld visitors such as the Beatles' Sergeant Pepperland will take place when it is not in use for staging shows or spectaculars.

As an integral part of the presentation there is to be a Hollywood Bowl type open-air auditorium. In the area, too, will be included a Rollerama, Disco and a sophisticated night spot. All to make sure the music goes on.

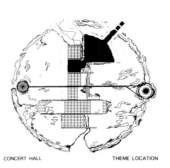

CONCERT HALL   THEME LOCATION

INGREDIENTS: CONCERT HALL
● Jeff Wayne's 'The War of the Worlds'
  Concert Hall
  Capsule Theatre Spectaculars
  Outdoor Arena
  Rollerama
  Discocavern
  Laserland
▲ Stargazers Night Club
  Jump Up Juice Bar
  Sunshine Rollerama Terrace
■ Major Emporia:
  Records
  Disco Equipment
  Recording Equipment
  Video Equipment
  Musical Instruments
  Music Memorabilia
  Books
  Musical Publications
◆ Box Office
  Preview Kiosk
  Service Facilities

Rock music . . .

Much more than music...

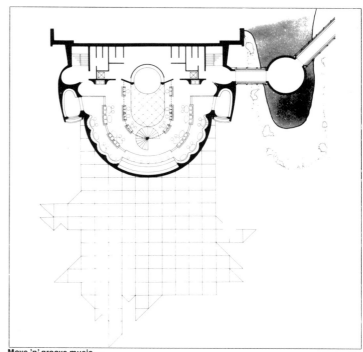

Move 'n' groove music...

Roll music...

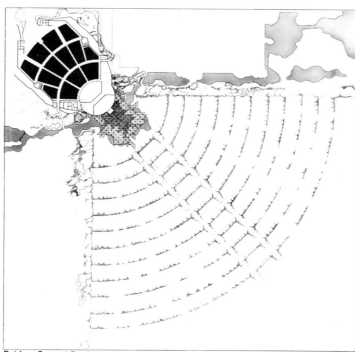

Outdoor Concert Bowl

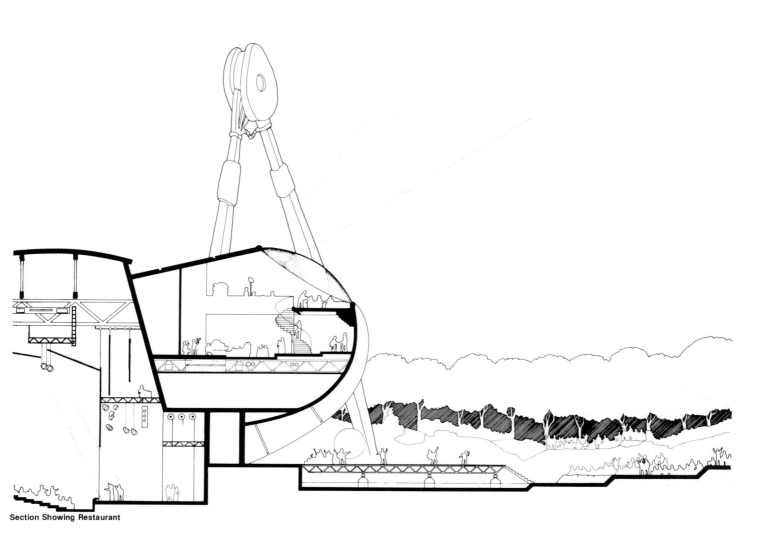

Section Showing Restaurant

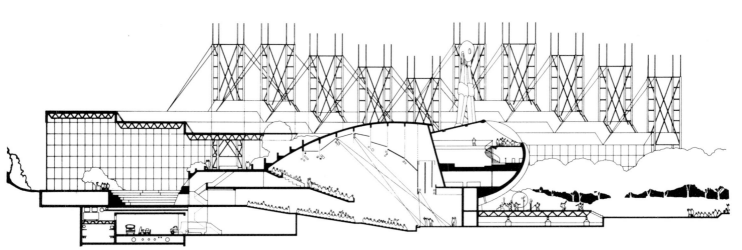

Concert Hall Section

THE WORLD: playing the game

The Wonderworld Game Plan for the World is a fascinating one that lets participants see how much, or how little, they know about the resources of the world they live in, and how they relate to us here in the United Kingdom. It's a highly sophisticated computerised affair consisting of a giant globe that comes to life before the players, each with their own individual game monitor which is used to answer questions put to them by the resident Master of Ceremonies.

But it is far more exciting than the normal quiz game. More educational too, as the subjects can vary from the location of minerals or other natural resources to the way we're affected by commerce, industry and invention. It's loosely based on Buckmaster Fuller's World Game but uses the technology and special effects to bring it right into the eighties.

Apart from the game itself there will be a feature on the computer in industry and the money market, in easy to understand language and an area where individual industries can showcase themselves in an attractive environment.

Another attraction will be the mad and the magnificent in British Science. Our history is coloured by genius from Heath Robinson to Isaac Newton, embracing contributions which have affected the well-being of people in Britain and elsewhere.

At Wonderworld the young inventors will also have an opportunity to demonstrate their genius, compete in competitions, get advice and be influenced by the best talents around.

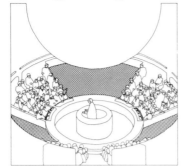

Play

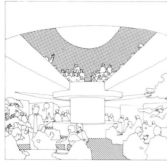

Rest

Showcasing British Industry

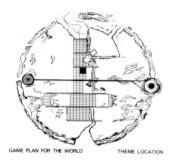

GAME PLAN FOR THE WORLD   THEME LOCATION

INGREDIENTS: WORLD
● **Game Plan for the World**
Industrial Computer Park
The Mad and the Magnificent of British Science
The Money Market
● **Wonderworld Schools Workshop**
▲ Industry Showcase
Exhibition Areas
■ International Food Facilities
International Emporium/World Market
Office Space
Banking Facilities
◆ Service Facilities

Wonderworld will encourage schools and provide resources and facilities for projects. The Southbrook School Add-a-car project, sponsored by B.P., is representative of the ambition.

Experience the mad and magnificent of British science.

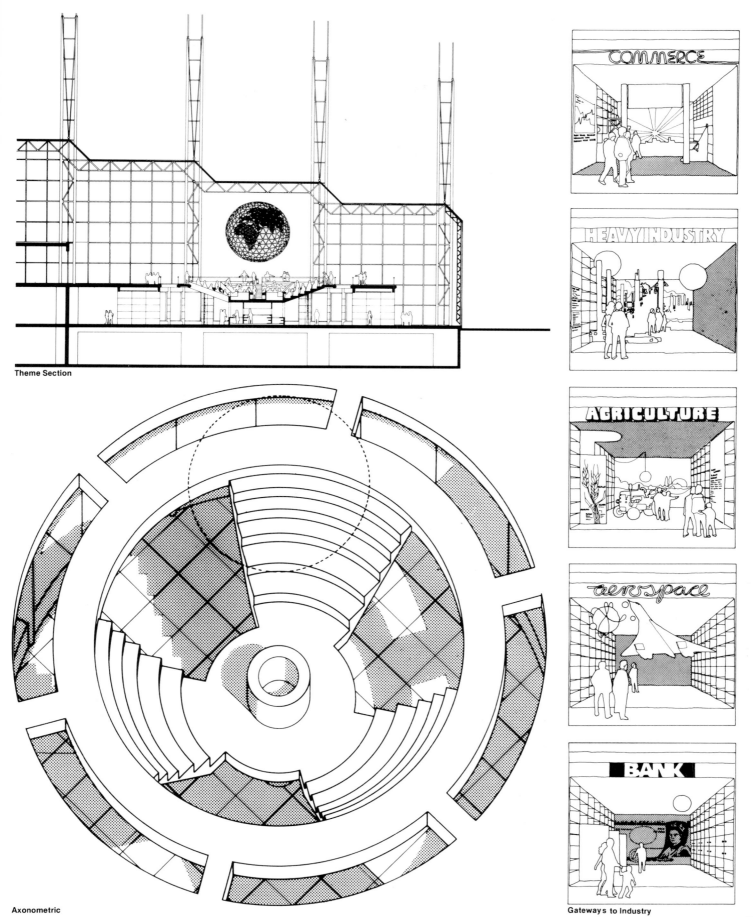

Theme Section

Axonometric

Gateways to Industry

COMMERCE

HEAVY INDUSTRY

AGRICULTURE

aerospace

BANK

37

The Rt. Hon. Sir John Eden Bt. MP

WonderWorld welcomes change

'Wonderworld' will help to prepare us for to-morrow by making us more aware of what is happening to-day.

At work, at home, at school, in hospital, shop and bank—the impact of microelectronics is revolutionising the way we do things and the amount of time that requires. Even if we have not all actually made use of the new technologies, most of us do at least know about the applications which are increasingly becoming a part of everyday life.

For example, we are all familiar with TV games, the video-recorder and satellite communications. Their benefit is clear. They add a new dimension to home entertainment and generally improve the quality of life. Developments in the office such as computers, data files, telex-machines, printers, word processors and so on are already part of the everyday scene. We have come to recognise how much they can help to increase throughput and improve efficiency. Similar advances have also long been part of manufacturing, where growing use is being made of numerically controlled machine tools, computer-aided design, robots and the like.

Yet all this is only the beginning. Bigger changes are on the way. Changes which will affect the whole pattern of living, altering fundamentally our approach to work and providing us with vast new opportunities for leisure.

It is essential that we know about what is to come, for unless we understand the implications for ourselves and our families we may fail to make the most of these immensely exciting developments. The more we know the less we will fear. To be afraid of the unknown is a perfectly natural but not particularly constructive reaction. By finding out what is going on and familiarising ourselves with the new technology, we will substantially broaden our own horizons and make it possible for our children to share more fully in the benefits that are emerging.

'Wonderworld' will help us to do this. By building on well-known scenes and figures from literature and from the past, by drawing on the services of popular characters from the present, and by creating a setting which though imaginatively futuristic is nonetheless within our everyday experience, the mystique will be taken out of microelectronics and we will come to see these things for what they really are: the means to a fuller life for us all.

New technology is not for the elite alone. The new technology is for Everyman.

Literally to bring that message home, 'Wonderworld' is to provide for individual participation and education for people of all ages from all parts of the country and beyond. By actually using the cameras or the computers, by actually experiencing the techniques of deep-sea exploration or by sampling the simulated thrills of space travel, as well as by more studies into the application of microelectronics at the shop-floor and work-bench, we will all be able to check for ourselves the relevance of these developments to our own lives.

And it will be fun.

This is not to be yet another inert dry-as-dust exhibition. It will be full of life and bustle and action, involving school children, old people, families, companies, societies—the whole community— in all the thrills of discovery as new vistas for leisure and entertainment are brought within our grasp. The golf course, sports centre, concert hall and other similar attractions are being designed to emphasise that education and entertainment are not mutually exclusive concepts. They complement each other. Both will be there, in combination, to serve our needs for the future.

New technology is also big business. Its growth potential has enormous significance for our total economic

strength. Whole new industries are being created, some spawned from groups established in North America or Japan, but many deriving from British research programmes which are already making an important contribution to the national wealth. British inventions and British technology are widely respected, but it is obviously right that we should be doing all we possibly can to stimulate their greater introduction into the home market, without which expanding penetration of overseas markets is more difficult to achieve.

'Wonderworld' will help us to welcome change, not to resist it.

It is not by accident that Group Five's brilliantly conceived project is to be located in an area once heavily dependent in economic and employment terms on one of the oldest and most basic of our industries, steel, which is itself now grappling with the problems of change. To their great credit, civic leaders in Corby are pointing the way. They can see the advantages of new technology for their people. And they are ready to seize them.

Without a positive attitude towards new developments we may get left behind. The advances will go on. Technology will not stand still as we cautiously examine whether there is anything in it for us. There will be no go-slow in technology while we hesitate or hold back. The changes will continue at an ever-increasing pace and we must quickly learn to come to terms with them.

We embrace the new technology readily enough when we can identify the immediate benefit to ourselves. It is understandably more difficult to accept new techniques, practices and attitudes when to do so requires the displacement of the old established way of doing things. Yet to lift the lid on what is already happening in microelectonics, telecommunications and computing is to reveal new and exciting developments that must increasingly influence our life at home, at work and at play.

For example, satellites will make available TV broadcasts covering the whole of Europe; optical-fibre communications lines could bring the equivalent of a complete library of books into the living room, computer-aided learning will extend the boundaries of the classroom in having a computer to 'teach' the pupil by question and answer; computer programmes will edit prose and correct bad English. At home computers will one day be as commonplace as the telephone is now; there will be more advanced forms of TV games in which the individual actually becomes part of and influences, the action; there will be instant 'mail-ordering' via the TV set; three-dimensional TV; computer-aided diagnosis and treatment in cases of ill-health. And much, much more.

'Wonderworld' will be the shop-window for them all. This will be an exciting 'adventure playground' for the whole family, giving to life a new dimension by bringing together in single beautifully-landscaped setting the many different aspects and applications of new technology. The British people will have the unique opportunity to learn about them, to experience them and to enjoy them—making to-morrow come alive for us all to-day.

RESORT AREA: never out of season

A beautiful, sparkling blue pool with waves that lap against a sandy, palm-fringed shore. An ideal place to take the 'sun'. On two sides of the pool the landscape is rocky, with seats carved into tiers that reach down to the water. This will be the centrepiece of the Wonderworld resort area.

It's been designed so that both the covered and open area can be used as one - depending on the time of year and the weather. Near the pool will be other attractions. For the children - adventure pools, slides, chutes and other wonderful things to do that will keep them happy for hours. Not to mention hot springs, rapids and diving tanks.

For those who want a change from all the water activities there's quite a choice. There's a fully equipped health club with a jacuzzi, sauna, solarium and luxuriously appointed dressing rooms. There are places, as well, where you'll be able to wander or just relax among lush plants and colourful flowers.

Refreshments will be available in a nearby cafeteria, suitably themed to fit in with the area's character and atmosphere.

The resort area will naturally be open to all park visitors, and those who are long-term guests will have a monorail link available to them direct from the hotel and hospitality zone.

Jack Nicklaus designed championship course and golf complex.

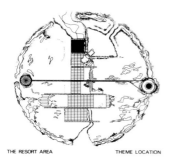
THE RESORT AREA   THEME LOCATION

INGREDIENTS: RESORT
● Wave Pool
Diving Tanks
Water Slides
Children's Pool
Sports Film Centre
Sports Simulators
Jack Nicklaus Golf Academy
Leisure Emporium
▲ Sportsman's Rest Restaurant
Promenade Cafeteria
◆ Service Facilities

Soak up the 'sun' whatever the season.

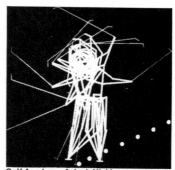
Golf Academy. A Jack Nicklaus master-class for all ages.

See what you score when you take penalties against a screened image of England's Peter Shilton.

Wonderworld—the sports centre for all sports.

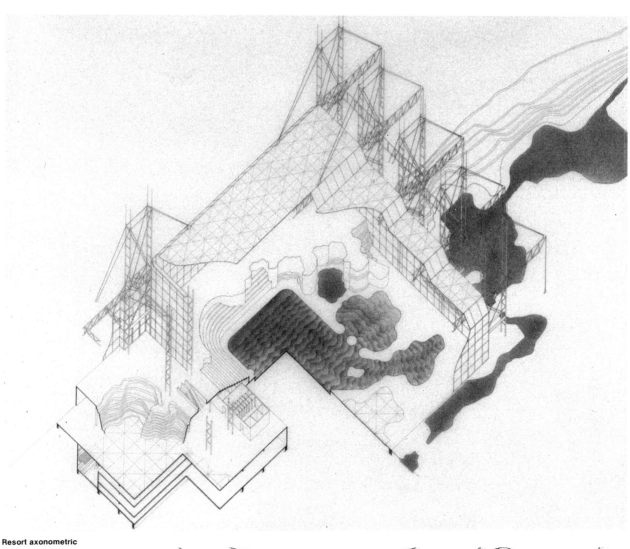

Resort axonometric

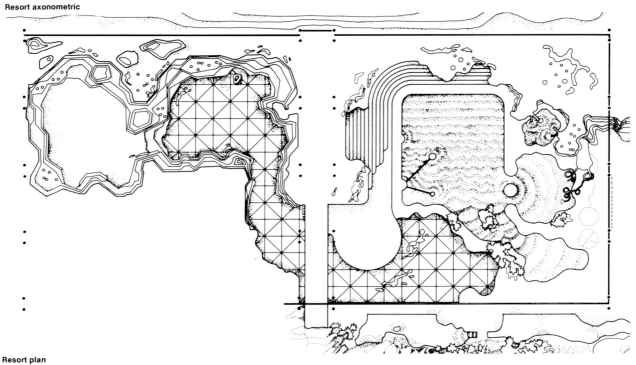

Resort plan

THE STADIUM: sport for all

Although presenting many unusual and exciting forms of recreation, Wonderworld hasn't neglected the conventional and popular activities. Which is why there will be a covered stadium accommodating 10,000 spectators in the heart of the sports complex.

Whilst this will be used for a wide variety of professional and amateur events, the emphasis will be very much on the participation angle. Its use will be dominated by coaching classes.

Nearby will be training pitches and playing fields that will offer superb facilities to all who wish to take advantage of them. Among the attractions will be the professional golf course, designed by and under the direction of Jack Nicklaus.

He will personally be formulating a programme that includes a golfing academy for players of all ages and standards - a place where one can practice and receive expert guidance.

Jack Nicklaus will be just one of the sporting personalities who will set the standards for sport at Wonderworld.

The stadium is roofed by a steel cable net, supported on a central steel ring and hung from 12 steel masts which are stayed back into the surrounding parking. The cladding is an inflated double membrane of Teflon coated glass fabric, giving good internal natural illumination, acoustic absorption and insulation against condensation for minimum weight (3 KG/M²).

Artificial lighting is from the roof and ventilation from the plant room beneath the seats.

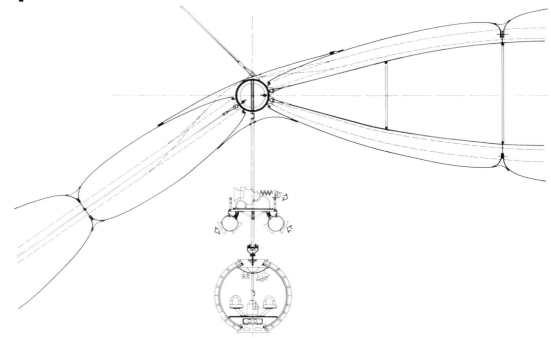

Construction Detail

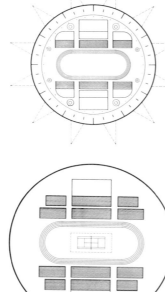

INGREDIENTS: THE STADIUM AND SPORTS PROGRAMME

● Covered Stadium
Athletics
Five-a-side Football
Equestrian Events
Gymnastics
Basketball
Volleyball
Indoor Hockey
Weightlifting
Boxing
Archery
Bowling
It's a Knockout
Book of Records HQ
Outdoor all-weather pitches
Racket Sports
Squash
Badminton
Tennis
Cricket, outdoor practice areas and indoor nets
Health Club
Gymnasium
▲ Fast Food and Resaurants
■ Sports Shop:
Equipment
Instruction
◆ Support and Services Facilities

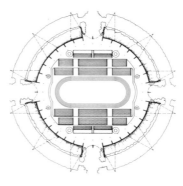

Tennis

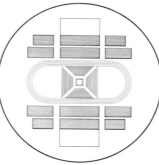

Boxing

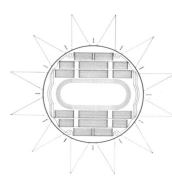

Gymnastics/Athletics

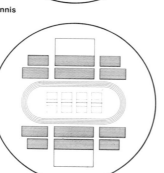

Volleyball

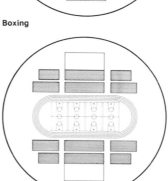

Basketball

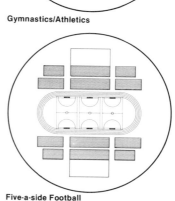

Five-a-side Football

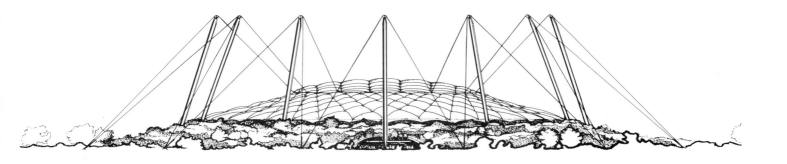

Elevation

Section and seating elevation

Section and interior terraces

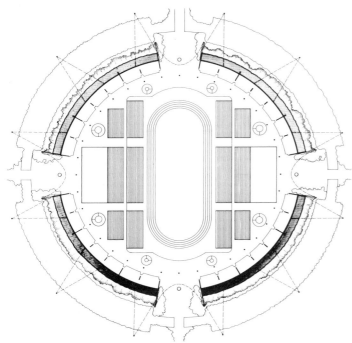

Ground floor plan

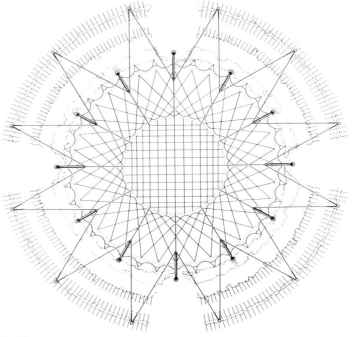

Roof plan

43

ENERGY: turn on

Few would disagree that one of the most important issues of today is the very real need to get the most out of our present energy supplies, as well as identifying and harnessing new sources.

Fortunately, those who provide our varied forms of fuel are proving themselves to be imaginative and dedicated in their quest for new energy forms, as well as in their efforts to make existing resources last as long as possible.

To tackle this awesome task they use all their skills, technology and invention to bring us the power we need to survive - but the responsibility should not be theirs alone. While the general public would agree that energy conservation is a 'good thing', it's true to say that all too often the individual lacks the motivation to do anything about it, even though hardly a day goes by without a reminder to be prudent with one of our most valuable commodities. Clearly there's a need to reinforce the existing educational programme.

At Wonderworld's Energy Pavilion there will be many dramatic demonstrations of energy in all its forms. Using the Wonderworld technique of visitor participation, a greater appreciation of the true situation and all of our social obligations will be put across in ways that will be remembered. For example, there's a computer energy game that awards players points for their efforts - and shows them how good (or bad) they are in life's energy game.

Omnimax Theatre. The Unforgettable experience.

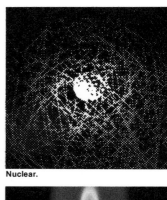

Nuclear.

Gas.

Electricity.

Oil.

Coal.

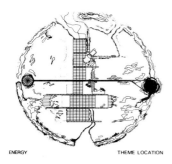

ENERGY   THEME LOCATION

INGREDIENTS: ENERGY
● Omnimax Theatre
  Energy Playground
  Energy Game
  Showcase: Energy Industry
▲ Monorail Station
  High Energy Food Bar
  Solar Soda
  Energy Emporium:
■ Books and Games
  Lighting
◆ Service Facilities

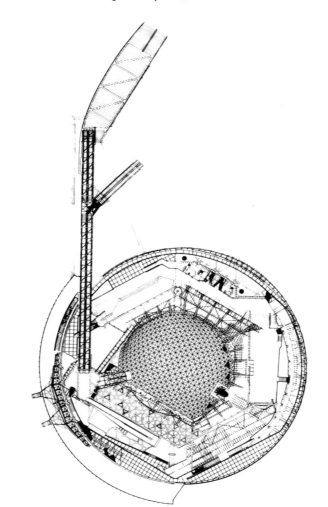

Energy pavilion plan

44

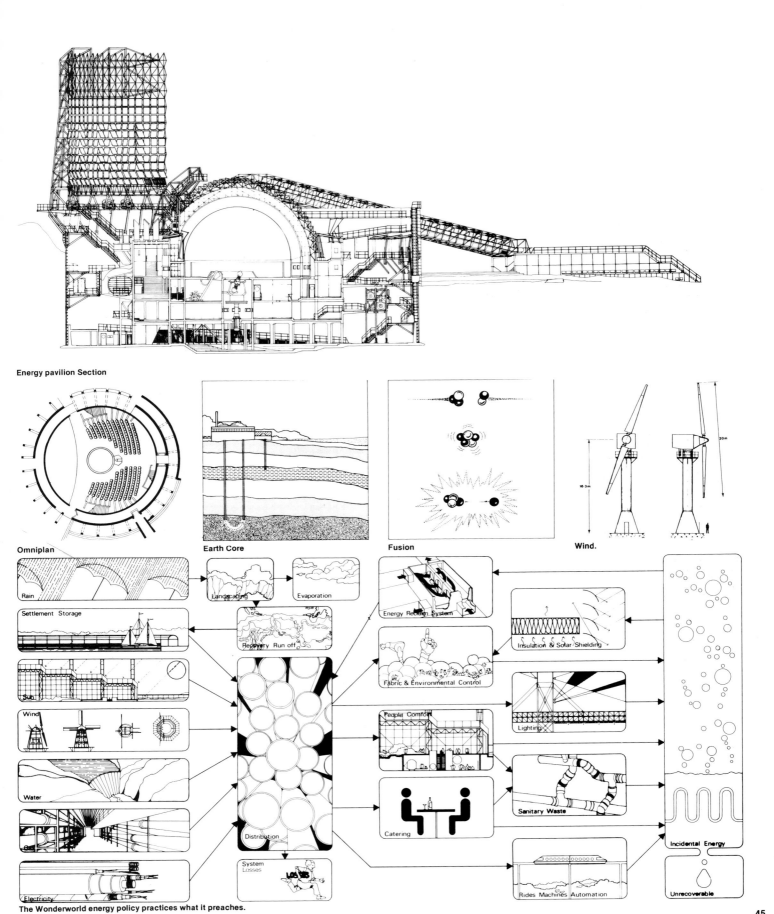

Energy pavilion Section

Omniplan

Earth Core

Fusion

Wind.

Rain

Landscaping

Evaporation

Settlement Storage

Recovery Run off

Energy Reclaim System

Insulation & Solar Shielding

Sun

Fabric & Environmental Control

Wind

People Comfort

Lighting

Water

Catering

Sanitary Waste

Electricity

Distribution

System Losses

Rides Machines Automation

Incidental Energy

Unrecoverable

The Wonderworld energy policy practices what it preaches.

SEA: in the wake of Drake

The sea has always had a special place in the hearts of Britons. It's the strong outer wall of our island defences, resisting every attempt to breach it since our emergence as a nation. For centuries we have taken a good harvest from, plundered upon, romanced about and sung of the sea, as well as founding an empire through our command of the oceans. Now we are discovering untold wealth beneath its bed.

Today's Drake to Queen Elizabeth II is the oil-company-privateer, returning to our shores with greater riches for the nation than Sir Francis ever did, as the result of bright, enterprising and bloodless maritime actions.

At Wonderworld the space-age sea world will prove to be a fabulous source of fun and education. Visitors will travel on a submarine journey that takes in the wonders of the deep and man's achievements there.
The main attraction is supported by many others, including a feature which provides the opportunity for a member of an audience to stand in the shoes of Nelson and command the fleet of miniature ships in a computer re-run of the Battle of Trafalgar. The Armada and Jutland would offer alternative programs.
The chance, too, will be given via simulators for visitors to fish with sonar... or land a helicopter onto an oil-rig pad during stormy weather.

The start of an underwater adventure.

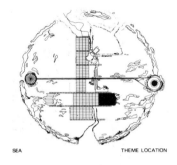

SEA   THEME LOCATION

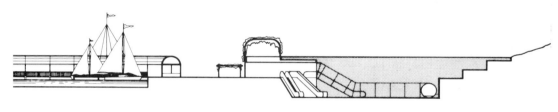

Sea Theme Section

INGREDIENTS: SEA
● North Sea Underwater Exploration
Sea Battles:
Jutland
Trafalgar
The Spanish Armada
'Salt Sings' Musical Hall
Aquarium Walkthrough
Aquarium Platform
Video Area
Boats and Boating Display
Jetty Walks
Moon Mooring
Fishing
▲ Fish and Chip Shop
Seafood Restaurant
Tiddlers Fast Fish
■ Emporium:
Fishing Tackle
Books
Corals
Fish
Wonderworld Rock and Candy
Ice Cream Parlour
Bamforth Photo Fantasy Booth
◆ Exhibition Facilities
Information
Service Facilities

Reconnoitre an oil-rig.

46

Sea Shell sensations.

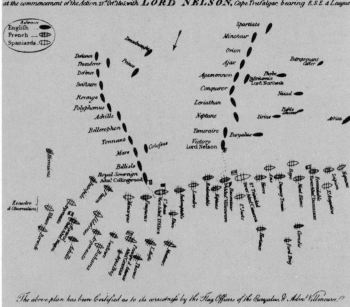

POSITION of the COMBINED FORCES of FRANCE & SPAIN, at the commencement of the Action 21.st Oct.t 1805 with LORD NELSON, Cape Trafalgar, bearing E.S.E. 4 Leagues

Stand in the shoes of Nelson and conduct the Battle of Trafalgar in a computer-run encounter.

An underwater walk-through aquarium that gives a fish-eye view of marine life.

'Salts sing!' A sea dogs, sea legs and sea shanties music hall.

Group Five

WonderWorld Design and Development

Guidelines

When contemplating the development of a new leisure facility it is important to plot accurately the economic and social charts which could affect its well-being, without being wrongly influenced by the temporary wrinkles in the graphs which may occur at any one time. It is also important to identify the immediate competition and consider how features could be assembled in exciting new combinations without duplication, compromise, or confusion in presentation and performance with rival places. It is therefore essential to prepare the ground and create a commercial foundation with sensible marketing parameters staked out as a discipline to govern subsequent decisions. Within these given constraints any proposed leisure development must demonstrate that it is desirable, financially viable, marketable, manageable - and buildable.

The Programme

The purpose of the design and development programme is to fashion the concept - the essence of the planned enterprise - up to the very point of implementation. The completed development programme will display in detail all disciplines and prospects, thereby defining and demonstrating the overall worth of the project and the likely growth pattern, for the benefit of authorities, investors and public.

Whilst acknowledging that this planned themepark is based upon the idea of educational fun, the development programme will show, for the benefit of each proprietor and covenanter seeking involvement, the prospects and anticipated returns. And for the authorities, the levels of employment and the many other benefits which will accrue to the local community will be demonstrated.

The early marketing and design work was undertaken to create a conceptual model which would attract the wide spread of talent required for such a development. The response from leading professionals in the UK and overseas has been most encouraging and the aim is for this process to continue so that the very best international skills can be incorporated in this themed dedication to Great Britain.

Under the following five key headings, each of which is an important part of the development, ever-expanding teams of professionals will contribute.

1. Emotional Factors

Themes, characters, concepts and ideas

This aspect is concerned with working up the thematic content already identified as seeming right and memorable in a grand presentation of our own nation - the very essence of Wonderworld and its related industries. A staged programme of evaluation, refinement and addition, purposely bringing together a wide range of robust characters, concepts, ideas and subjects. Together they'll produce a presentation with popular and specialist appeals.

Any company undertaking the development of a themepark can have no better living example than Disney World to emulate. Valuable information plucked from Disney World supplies many of the disciplines and designs for a new themepark.

It can be expected that a company with a serious ambition would be able to set out a plan, based upon the legitimate education gained by observing a quite extraordinary and admirable performance by Disney.

However, the one magical ingredient no one can take from Disney World is the fabulous characterisation of Mickey Mouse and the rest.

Without characters, any new themepark, however well-conceived and developed in all other respects, will be cripplingly deficient overall.

The developers of Wonderworld acknowledge that Disney characters play a relatively minor role within the confines of Disney World itself, but only schemes obsessively focused solely on the physical presentation of a themepark could underrate their strategic importance.

The reason that manufacturing companies have entered into highly profitable relationships with Disney is not because of the Disney parks as a whole, but rather because of Donald Duck.

48

WonderWorld ©

A themepark demands that people make the effort to journey to it, whereas appealing characters will filter their way into people's homes regardless, acting as a fifth column sales force drumming up interest and themepark business around the globe.

2. Physical Factors

Location, planning, architecture, engineering, specialist design, construction and set design

These are disciplines by which the individual ideas and themes develop their own appearance and presentation as features within the themepark - their physical look, the parts to be co-ordinated within the concept of the overall plan. The relationship between each of the different themes in the context of the grand plan is of vital importance, and will exert enormous influence upon performance and the levels of administration required. In all, the physical factors will determine customer convenience and, probably most important of all, the visual impact of the place.

3. Management Factors

Organisation and operating levels

It will be necessary to create the right management structure and develop a manpower policy. This is particularly important as a themepark is a people business with high levels of visits and high ratios of people supplying a service. Key management personnel will be identified during the development programme and the levels of staffing will be determined for the planned growth pattern of Wonderworld. Seasonal fluctuations, employment of permanent and part-time staff (professional and manual) are some of the factors that have to be taken into account.

4. Marketing Factors

Research, P.R., promotion, ancillary product and merchandising

Research
The work of gathering data and monitoring the American themeparks will carry on. Research studies will continue to be commissioned from a number of different and independent research organisations as an aid to management judgement.

Method of Concept Evaluation
i) Management Appraisal Filter
Rationalised and realised in appreciable forms, the concepts need to demonstrate their appeal to the management in judgement. Those concepts that gain approval will be subjected to the Consumer Evaluation Filter.

ii) Consumer Evaluation Filter
Groups of consumers representative of the socio-economic candidature have been reviewing the options. Only those concepts proving themselves worthy (be they those with a particular but sufficient appeal, or those able to muster strong general support) can justify pairing with the most ideal sponsor drawn from carefully compiled lists of blue chip company candidates. With the active cooperation of the most favoured and responsive company in each case, customised strategic, economic and feasibility criteria may be set.
This will provide an essential basis for converting the concepts into a fully developed proposal detailing content, design, supply, construction, cost, rate of return, etc. - a proposition in dimension, ready for feeding into the Economic and Feasibility Analysis Filter.

iii) Economic and Feasibility Analysis Filter
This stage determines whether the developed proposal meets

the sound economic and feasibility parameters previously set, especially where the original brief has been extended, as a result of new opportunities arising.

After adjustments and refinements and subject to a second check by management, consumers, researchers and analysis, the customised presentation (which is the joint product of both the company's own executives and the Wonderworld development team) shall be submitted to the company's board for their consideration.

iv) Sponsor's Evaluation Filter

This stage enables the management of the prospective covenanter company to review the proposal in respect of their own policies and to assess it against any other relevant opportunity. Given the commitment of the company, both managements will work together to implement the plan.

Promotion and Publicity

Careful control is being exercised on the volume and direction of publicity - to pace rather than precede developments. Committees will monitor progress throughout the development. Amongst these will be one comprising experts on those interests and subjects portrayed in the themepark, whilst another will attend to the political needs and general well-being of the development.

Ancillary Product and Merchandising

A themepark will only prove successful if it opens in a grand climate of awareness, which is the acknowledgement that both the product and the promise must be clearly understood and enthusiastically approved by sufficient numbers to justify itself.

This is a precondition of sale that applies to any new product introduction which is aiming for broad-scale appeal and patronage to justify heavy up-front investment. The slow-burn tease and equally slow word-of-mouth campaigns offer no alternative.

The healthy climate that existed around Disneyland at the time of its opening serves as a positive example. Long before the first stone of the park was laid, the Disney imagery had been sold successfully. This is not to suggest that his cartoon characters were conceived as a powerful and far-sighted promotional campaign and that the park was their purpose - but the impact was the same as if they had been. When the time came for Disneyland's opening, most people knew about it and what it promised. The majority wanted what it offered and all knew exactly where to find it. Not only had the Disney organisation successfully pre-sold the park, but instead of that vast promotional campaign being another drain on the development budget, the exercise was profit-making.

The aim is to nurture the growth of the theme with the public in such a way that the subsequent appearance of the themepark and its flowering will be the celebrated natural development. By following this, the Disney route, we can be assured that the park will open -importantly - in a climate of complete awareness. The syndication of comic strips, the publication of educational and other books, and the manufacture of toys are typical examples of the items that are currently being developed.

5. Economic Factors

Economic feasibility. Capital requirements. Return on capital. Covenanter contributions. Working capital requirements for merchandising, etc.

The financial needs of the development programme will be established after careful and calculated assessment of the requirements and prospects of the total enterprise in all of its parts. These aspects will include:

★Capital cost projections including:

i)   Themepark pavilions, rides, exhibitions and common areas.
ii)   Infrastructure - general.
iii) Golf course.
iv)   Hotel and hospitality facilities.

★Working capital costs for sources of income include:
i)   Preliminary merchandising.